What people are saying about

Frank Viola's Books

From Eternity to Here

"*From Eternity to Here* is a masterpiece. A must-read for those who believe and for others who want to believe. It reads like a movie on paper."

Dr. Myles Munroe, pastor and author of
Rediscovering the Kingdom and *God's Big Idea*

"Frank continues to challenge the church-at-large with a powerful mind, an impassioned voice, and a love for the bride of Christ. You need to get this book and wrestle with Frank through the biblical passages regarding our identity in Christ as His body and the mission our God has entrusted to us."

Ed Stetzer, coauthor of
Breaking the Missional Code (www.edstetzer.com)

"As Viola unfolds the glorious story of God's quest for a bride, readers will find their imaginations inspired and their lives transformed. The sheer beauty of God's magnificent plan compels our allegiance and revolutionizes our lives. This retelling of the 'old, old story' is a much-needed gift to the church today."

Greg Boyd, pastor, theologian, and author of
Letters from a Skeptic, Myth of a Christian Nation, and *God at War*

Reimagining Church

"In *Reimagining Church*, Frank Viola is at the top of his game, showing a serene, soaring mastery of the theology of church as organism rather than organization."

Leonard Sweet, author of
Soul Tsunami, 11, and *So Beautiful*

"Dissent is a gift to the church. It is the imagination of the prophets that continually call us back to our identity as the peculiar people of God. May Viola's words challenge us to become the change that we want to see in the church … and not to settle for anything less than God's dream for her."

Shane Claiborne, author of *The Irresistible Revolution,*
activist, and recovering sinner (thesimpleway.org)

"True to form, this book contains a thoroughly consistent critique of prevailing forms of church. However, in *Reimagining Church*, Frank Viola also presents a positive vision of what the church can become if we truly reembraced more organic, and less institutional, forms of church. This is a no-holds-barred prophetic vision for the church in the twenty-first century."

Alan Hirsch, missional strategist and author of
The Forgotten Ways

FINDING
ORGANIC
CHURCH

A COMPREHENSIVE GUIDE TO STARTING
—————— ## AND SUSTAINING ——————
AUTHENTIC CHRISTIAN COMMUNITIES

FRANK VIOLA

transforming lives together

FINDING ORGANIC CHURCH
Published by David C. Cook
4050 Lee Vance View
Colorado Springs, CO 80918 U.S.A.

David C. Cook Distribution Canada
55 Woodslee Avenue, Paris, Ontario, Canada N3L 3E5

David C. Cook U.K., Kingsway Communications
Eastbourne, East Sussex BN23 6NT, England

David C. Cook and the graphic circle C logo
are registered trademarks of Cook Communications Ministries.

The Web site addresses recommended throughout this book are offered as a
resource to you. These Web sites are not intended in any way to be or imply an
endorsement on the part of David C. Cook, nor do we vouch for their content.

All Scripture quotations, unless otherwise noted, are taken from the *Holy Bible,
New International Version*. *NIV*. Copyright © 1973, 1978, 1984 by International
Bible Society. Used by permission of Zondervan. All rights reserved. Scripture
quotations marked NASB are taken from the *New American Standard Bible*, ©
Copyright 1960, 1995 by The Lockman Foundation. Used by permission; NKJV are
taken from the New King James Version. Copyright © 1982 by Thomas Nelson,
Inc. Used by permission. All rights reserved; MSG are taken from *THE MESSAGE*.
Copyright © by Eugene H. Peterson 1993, 1994, 1995, 1996, 2000, 2001, 2002.
Used by permission of NavPress Publishing Group; KJV are taken from the King
James Version of the Bible. (Public Domain); and ESV are taken from *The Holy
Bible, English Standard Version*. Copyright © 2000; 2001 by Crossway Bibles, a
division of Good News Publishers. Used by permission. All rights reserved.

LCCN 2009929670
ISBN 978-1-4347-6866-7
eISBN 978-0-7814-0352-8

Published in association with the literary agency of Daniel Literary
Group, 1701 Kingsbury Dr., Ste. 100, Nashville, TN 37215

The Team: Don Pape, John Blase, Amy Kiechlin,
Sarah Schultz, Jack Campbell, and Karen Athen
Cover Design: Tim Green, The DesignWorks Group
Cover Illustration: Connie Gabbert, The DesignWorks Group

Printed in the United States of America
First Edition 2009

1 2 3 4 5 6 7 8 9 10

061709

To all church planters of the past who counted the cost,
forged the path, and showed the way ... and to a
future generation of young men and women
called of God who will stand on their
shoulders and see further
than they did

CONTENTS

PART FOUR
PULLING THE WEEDS—HEALTH AND DEVELOPMENT

PREFACE

Since I've been writing about organic church life, people have consistently asked me two questions: (1) Where can I find the type of church that you write about? and (2) How does one plant an organic church?

This book is an attempt to answer both questions in a comprehensive way.

The principles set forth are not untested theories. You will not find armchair philosophy or bloodless abstractions within these pages.

Rather, the principles described have been hammered out on the anvil of experience—both positive and negative. They have been discovered through many mistakes (a good number of which are my own) as well as a number of accidental successes. They are also supported by the voice of Scripture.

I have often described myself as an observing biologist. For the last twenty-one years, I've watched organic church life take root. I've observed how it functions, what nurtures it, and what chokes it.

I will shamelessly admit that I don't possess all the answers. I'm still in school. I'm still watching the glories and gores of organic church life. I'm also still experimenting. I don't believe there are any experts in this business—only a catalog of failures and successes.

This book, then, is an attempt to present a theology of organic church planting, along with a number of practical helps for those who wish to embark on this journey.

Since I've been a Christian, I've made a number of observations regarding the problems endemic to the contemporary church—both traditional and nontraditional. These experiences have led me to the following conclusions:

1. Most churches, including a large number of house churches and simple churches, have strayed far afield from the *experience* of the body of Christ. The chief reason being that we have largely ignored what Scripture has to say about God's way of planting churches.

2. Many of the problems germane to both traditional and nontraditional churches could be resolved if we returned to the biblical witness of church planting and nurturing.

Granted, these conclusions are built on pragmatic observations. But they also carry the weight of Scripture to support them. And they are the motivation that provoked this book.

Four books precede this one in a series I've written on radical church restoration. *The Untold Story of the New Testament Church* is a narrative ecclesiology, rehearsing the story of the New Testament church in chronological order. *Pagan Christianity* (coauthored with

George Barna) traces the origins of our modern church practices. It demonstrates that most of our traditional church practices are without biblical merit and out of sync with the organic nature of the church.

Reimagining Church presents a living-color image of New Testament church life for the twenty-first century.[1] It's a detailed theology of organic church for our time. *From Eternity to Here* explores the eternal purpose of God—the grand mission that ought to govern our church life as well as our spiritual service. It presents the big sweeping epic of God's ultimate passion.

The book you hold in your hands picks up where *From Eternity to Here, Reimagining Church, Pagan Christianity,* and *The Untold Story of the New Testament Church* leave off. It takes a detailed look at how an organic expression of the church is born in a given place and how it can be sustained.

I highly recommend that you read the previous four books along with this one because many questions pertinent to the topic of organic church are answered therein. This book stands as the fifth in the series.

Throughout this volume, I'll be using the following terms interchangeably: *church planter, apostle, Christian worker, itinerant worker,* and *apostolic worker.* I will explain my reasoning for this later in the book. I'll also be using the term *he* to describe apostles. Not because I believe that only men can be apostolic workers, but merely because it's simpler to write "he" than "he or she." (I have no problem with the idea that women can engage in apostolic work.

---

1   It should be noted that I am using the word *church* throughout this volume as it is used in the New Testament. "Church" is not a building, a denomination, or a religious service. Rather, "church"—translated from the Greek word *ekklesia*—embodies two ideas: *community* and *assembly.* The New Testament envisions the church as a close-knit *community* whose members share God's life and *assemble* together regularly.

Junia is listed as an apostle in Romans 16:7, and Priscilla and Phoebe were a great asset to Paul's apostolic ministry.)[2]

That said, I have written this book for three different audiences.

First, it is written for those who wish to begin meeting in an organic way and would like some practical help for the journey.

Second, it is written for the scores of people who are involved in missional churches, incarnational churches, relational churches, emerging churches, house churches, simple churches, and even organic churches. (These are not synonyms; there are distinctions between each.)

Third, it is written for every person who feels called to plant churches—no matter what type.

The book is divided up into four parts. Part 1 explores the spiritual principles that govern church planting in the New Testament. Part 2 answers common objections to the points made in part 1. Part 3 is a practical guide for beginning an organic church. And part 4 deals with the health and development of organic churches. The footnotes supply detailed information as to how I came to various conclusions as well as source citations. I'm well aware that the paradigm shift that this book calls for will be hard for many mainstream thinkers to absorb. Yet I appeal to Scripture, experience, and New Testament scholarship to buttress my views, and I hope that my readers will seriously consider them.

In this connection, it's my contention that most Christians are stuck in the prevailing paradigms that dominate the religious world today.[3] Let me illustrate with a historical example.

---

2   See Eldon Jay Epp, *Junia: The First Woman Apostle* (Minneapolis, MN: Fortress, 2005). See also chapter 11 of this book and Acts 18:2–3, 18–19; 24ff.; Rom. 16:1–4, 7; 1 Cor. 16:19.

3   A paradigm is the overall understanding or model that is accepted by an intellectual community. A paradigm shift refers to a drastic change in that understanding or model.

In the mid-twentieth century, Swiss watchmakers had cornered the world market share for watches. But that changed when one of their own countrymen came out with a revolutionary new idea: *the quartz watch.*

Ironically, when the idea of the quartz watch was presented to the Swiss manufacturers, they laughed at it. They concluded that it could never work, so they refused to patent the idea. Seiko Watch Corporation, on the other hand, took one look at the quartz watch, and the rest is history.

The power of a prevailing paradigm had so influenced the Swiss watch manufacturers that they couldn't understand the new concept of the quartz watch. Because the watch had no gears, no mainspring, and no bearings, they rejected it. Their present paradigm didn't allow for the new innovation. The net effect was that they lost the leading edge on watchmaking, and they were forced to lay off thousands of workers. It was all because the quartz watch didn't fit into their worldview. It didn't map to their paradigm. They didn't appreciate the new way because they were blinded by the old way.

In the same manner, I'm convinced that a paradigm shift concerning the practice of the church *and* church planting is needed if the body of Christ will be restored to God's original intention. Note that a recovery of both church *practice* and church *planting* are needed. And both elements must be kept together. As Roland Allen once put it,

> *People have adopted fragments of St. Paul's method*
> *and have tried to incorporate them into alien systems,*

and the failure which resulted has been used as an argument against the Apostle's method.[4]

What is needed is a recovery of New Testament church-planting principles *to produce* New Testament–based churches. Put another way, we need a restoration of the divine pattern for church planting in order to produce organic churches. Consequently, an entirely new paradigm must be embraced for both church practice and church planting. Again, Allen writes,

> *It would be difficult to find any better model than the Apostle [Paul] in the work of establishing new churches. At any rate this much is certain, that the Apostle's methods succeeded exactly where ours have failed.*[5]

The rediscovery of the scriptural approach to church planting is an explosive dynamic that has the power to break traditional thinking and practice. For this reason, I pray that my readers will open their hearts wide to behold a new way—which is really an ancient way, handcrafted by God Himself.

Frank Viola
Gainesville, Florida
February 2009

---

4   Roland Allen, *Missionary Methods: St. Paul's or Ours?* (Grand Rapids, MI: Eerdmans, 1962), 5.
5   Roland Allen, *Missionary Methods: St. Paul's or Ours?* (Grand Rapids, MI: Eerdmans, 1962), 147.

INTRODUCTION

RECLAIMING THE BIBLICAL NARRATIVE

> *It is the depravity of institutions and movements that given in the beginning to express life, they often end in throttling that very life. Therefore, they need constant review, perpetual criticism and continuous bringing back to the original purposes and spirit. The Christian church is no exception. It is the chief illustration of the above.*
>
> —E. Stanley Jones

The purpose of this book is very simple: to present the biblical narrative for church planting and to reclaim that narrative for our day.

Origin Determines Destiny

The Bible puts a great deal of stress on origins. This is because in spiritual things, origin determines destiny. Therefore, the origin of a church will determine its destiny as well as its quality. Put another way, *how* a church is planted has a profound effect on the character, the effectiveness, and the future of that church. Consider Paul's words:

> *I planted the seed, Apollos watered it, but God made it grow. So neither he who plants nor he who waters is anything, but only God, who makes things grow. The man who plants and the man who waters have one purpose, and each will be rewarded according to his own labor. For we are God's fellow workers; you are God's field, God's building. By the grace God has given me, I laid a foundation as an expert builder, and someone else is building on it. But each one should be careful how he builds. For no one can lay any foundation other than the one already laid, which is Jesus Christ. If any man builds on this foundation using gold, silver, costly stones, wood, hay or straw, his work will be shown for what it is, because the Day will bring it to light. It will be revealed with fire, and the fire will test the quality of each man's work. (1 Cor. 3:6–13)*

In this passage, Paul uses two metaphors to describe the work of church planting: planting a field and constructing a building. For Paul, church planters are farmers (they "plant" the church), and they are builders (they "build" the church).

It is from this passage that the term *church planter* is derived. A church planter is one who plants the seed, which is the gospel of Jesus Christ, out of which a church is born. On the term *church planter*, Charles Brock writes,

> *The term "church planter" is rather new to many people. A church planter is a person, national or foreigner, who sows the gospel seed in a way that a New Testament church comes to life and grows.*[1]

Paul depicts the church as a field. But he also envisions it as a building. Yet it's a building that is alive. When Paul speaks of a field, he's not talking about an acre of dirt. He's speaking of a cultivated field such as a field of wheat.[2] Consequently, both metaphors have in view the organic nature of the church. The church is a *living* organism.

Within this passage, Paul mentions three ingredients for planting healthy churches:

1. The competence of the one who plants/builds the church.

> *By the grace God has given me, I laid a foundation as an expert builder. (1 Cor. 3:10a)*

2. The materials used for building.

---

1 Charles Brock, *The Principles and Practice of Indigenous Church Planting* (Nashville, TN: Broadman, 1981), 12–13.

2 The Greek word used in this passage literally means "a cultivated field." Interestingly, the New Testament is consistent in portraying wheat as a depiction of Christ and His people (John 12:24; 4:35; Mark 4:29; Luke 10:2).

If any man builds on this foundation using gold,
silver, costly stones, wood, hay or straw, his work will
be shown for what it is.… It will be revealed with fire,
and the fire will test the quality of each man's work.
(1 Cor. 3:12–13)

3. The way in which the church is built.

But each one should be careful how he builds. (1 Cor.
3:10b)

The Mechanical vs. the Organic

Tragically, many modern Christians have the benighted idea that starting a church is like assembling Lego blocks. One simply has to stick his nose in the Bible, extract from its pages the practices of the early church, imitate them, and voilà, a floatable "New Testament church" is created. I call this mechanical method of church formation "biblical blueprintism."

Biblical blueprintism is built on a rather thin ecclesiology and a misunderstanding of the organic nature of church life. For this reason, it's profoundly flawed.

An authentic church cannot be started by the bare hands of human beings—no more than a woman can be constructed through human ingenuity or imitation. A woman must be given birth. And once born, she must be nurtured to the point where she develops on her own.

Forgive the crass illustration, but lashing together two female arms and legs onto a torso and propping a female head on top will never produce a girl. To the naked eye such a concoction may resemble a human being. But it will always lack the essential quality of humanness—which is *life*. And life is the product of birth. This principle holds true when we consider the matter of church planting.

Consequently, the "biblical blueprint" model is rooted in the notion that the New Testament is the new Leviticus. Advocates approach the Bible like an engineer approaches an engineering textbook. Study the structural principles and then apply them.

But church planting is not a form of engineering. And the New Testament isn't a rule book. It's a record of the DNA of the church at work. As T. Austin-Sparks says,

> *The fact is that, while certain things characterized the New Testament churches, the New Testament does not give us a complete pattern according to which churches are to be set up or formed! There is no blueprint for churches in the New Testament, and to try to form New Testament churches is only to create another system which may be as legal, sectarian, and dead as others. Churches, like the Church, are organisms which spring out of life, which life itself springs out of the Cross of Christ wrought into the very being of believers. Unless believers are crucified people, there can be no true expression of the Church.*[3]

---

3   T. Austin-Sparks, *Words of Wisdom and Revelation* (St. Charles, MO: Three Brothers, 1971), 62.

For us humans, the family is genetic to our species. There will always be a father, a mother, and children. This cannot be broken. It's written in the arteries of creation.

In the same way, organic church life—the *experience* of the body of Christ—is instinctive to our species as Christians. It's woven into the bloodstream of God's universe. Provided that certain raw ingredients are in place, body life will organically and spontaneously break forth in the midst of a group of believers.

The problem we face is in removing all the baggage so that body life can arise naturally and stay healthy. This puts us on a collision course with the biblical principles of church planting.

What Is an Organic Church?

As I have stated elsewhere, I've been using this term for over fifteen years now. Today it has become somewhat of a clay word, being molded and shaped to mean a variety of different things by a variety of different people.

By *organic church*, I mean a church that is born out of spiritual life instead of being constructed by human institutions and held together by religious programs. Organic church life is a grassroots experience that is marked by face-to-face community, every-member functioning, open-participatory meetings (as opposed to pastor-to-pew services), nonhierarchical leadership, and the centrality and supremacy of Jesus Christ as the functional Leader and Head of the gathering.

By contrast, whenever we sin-scarred mortals try to create a church the same way we would start a business, we are defying the organic nature of church life. An organic church is one that is *naturally* produced when a group of people has encountered Jesus Christ in reality (external ecclesiastical props being unnecessary) and the DNA of the church is free to work without hindrance. It's the difference between standing in front of a fan and standing outdoors on a windy day.

To summarize, an organic church is not a theater with a script. It's a lifestyle—an authentic journey with the Lord Jesus and His disciples.

The difference between organic churches and nonorganic churches is the difference between General Motors and a vegetable garden. One is founded by humans, the other is birthed by God. One is artificial, the other is living.

For this reason, church planters are like farmers and midwives.

PART ONE
PLANTING THE SEED— BIBLICAL PRINCIPLES FOR CHURCH PLANTING

CHAPTER 1

THE DIVINE PATTERN OF CHURCH FORMATION

> *We must return to the beginning, to the "genesis" of the church, to see what He said and did then. It is there we find the highest expression of His will. Acts is the "genesis" of the church's history, and the church in the time of Paul is the "genesis" of the Spirit's work. Conditions in the church today are vastly different from what they were then, but these present conditions could never be our example, or our authoritative guide; we must return to the "beginning." Only what God has set forth as our example in the beginning is the eternal will of God.*

—Watchman Nee

Over the last fifty years, there have been nearly one hundred books written on the subject of church planting. Some of these books have the subject nailed down to a fine science. But what is surprising is that few of them discuss the ways in which churches were planted in the beginning.

To my mind, it's a profound mistake to ignore what we find in the book of Acts concerning the manner in which Christian communities were birthed in the first century. As Watchman Nee writes,

> *Never let us regard these early chapters of Acts as inapplicable today. Like the book of Genesis, the Acts of the Apostles reveals the beginnings of God's ways, and what He did then sets a pattern for His work always.*[1]

The New Testament presents four ways in which churches were planted in century one. These ways weren't cultural fads or the nifty ideas of intelligent mortals. I believe they originated with God Himself.

The Jerusalem Model

The first way occurred in the city of Jerusalem. Twelve apostles planted one church by the preaching of Jesus Christ (Acts 2:14—8:3). After a period of time, the church multiplied by "transplantation" or "migration."[2]

Because this approach began first in Jerusalem, we'll call it the *Jerusalem Model.* According to the New Testament narrative, after

---

1   Watchman Nee, *Church Affairs* (Richmond, VA: Christian Fellowship Publishers, 1982), 7.

2   Note that the images of *planting* and *transplantation* are that of organic farming. This is because the church is an organic, biotic life (1 Cor. 3:6–8; 12:1ff.).

four years, the seeds of the Jerusalem church were scattered and transplanted all throughout Palestine.[3] Because of persecution, the believers in Jerusalem relocated to other locales, shared their faith, and churches sprang up as a result (Acts 8:1–8; 11:19–21). For a time, the twelve apostles remained in the city.[4]

One of the outstanding characteristics of the Jerusalem dispersion is that all the Christians in Jerusalem had experienced organic church life *before* they relocated to form new churches. In other words, they brought to other regions their experience of Christ and the church. This is a vital point as we will later see.

Significantly, the newly transplanted churches in Palestine received the help of the apostles—even though they were not directly planted by them. The Twelve circulated to the new church plants, watering the seeds and pulling up weeds (Acts 9:32—11:30). While the apostles helped establish and encourage these new churches, they did not live in them, nor did they control their affairs.

The Antioch Model

The classic way in which churches were planted in the first century began in Antioch of Syria. This model of church planting is most clearly seen in Acts 13:1—20:38. Here we discover that Paul and his coworkers were sent out from Antioch to establish churches in South Galatia, Greece, and Asia Minor. This way of planting churches

---

3   All chronological dating used in this book is based on the research in my book *The Untold Story of the New Testament Church*.

4   Keep in mind that while the twelve apostles did not leave the city of Jerusalem for many years, the church in Jerusalem was extremely large. It numbered in the thousands. Consequently, this new church called for over ten apostles to establish the ground floor. All of these factors make Jerusalem, the first church on earth, unique.

can be called the *Antioch Model*. It can also be called "fresh seed planting."[5]

(Incidentally, Paul's journeys are best described as "church planting trips" or "apostolic journeys." The popular term *missionary journey* was created in the nineteenth century and is a poor fit with the nature and goal of Paul's ministry.[6] More on that later.)

The *Antioch Model* can be described thusly: An apostle walks bare-handed into a city to preach Jesus Christ. He does not preach the "Four Spiritual Laws," the "Romans road," the "plan of salvation," or Christian theology. Nor does he preach himself (2 Cor. 4:5). Instead, he preaches a Person—*Jesus Christ.*[7]

New converts are made as a result of the preaching of Christ. Some of them may be religious people who have a relationship with God already (the Jews). Others have never met God (the Gentiles).

After leading people into a genuine encounter with God in Christ, the apostle shows the young church how to live by the indwelling life of its newly found Lord. He discloses to the believers the eternal purpose of God, and this becomes the church's consuming vision.

---

5   Some have called this method "catalytic church planting." Others have called it "the Antioch line" of planting churches.

6   The term *missionary journey* finds its origin in nineteenth-century German commentaries on Paul. It was probably influenced by the fact that the eighteenth and nineteenth centuries saw the rise of world missionary work coupled with the economic exploitation of India, Africa, the Orient, and elsewhere by Europeans. (The commentaries of A. Schlatter confirm this.) As far as I know, the earliest reference to *missionary journey* in English is in David Thomas's *A Homiletic Commentary on the Acts of the Apostles* published in 1870. The word *mission* was not used to refer to human outreach until the sixteenth century. Before that time, it was used to refer to the sending of Jesus by the Father and the sending of the Spirit by the Father and Son (John 17:18). The Jesuits were the first to use the term *mission* to refer to the spreading of the Christian faith. In time, the word *mission* came to refer to the sending of people across frontiers to propagate the Christian faith, convert the heathens, plant churches, and improve society (R. Paul Stevens, *The Abolition of the Laity* [Carlisle, PA: Paternoster, 1999], 192).

7   See Acts 2:22–36; 8:5, 12, 35; 9:17–20; 10:38–43; 11:19–20; 17:2–3; Rom. 16:25; Gal. 3:1; 1 Cor. 2:2; 2 Cor. 4:5.

(Note that God's eternal purpose—His grand mission—is God-centered, not human-centered.) In short, the apostle imparts into the spirits of the believing community the same "heavenly vision" that he himself has received (Acts 26:13; Gal. 1:15–16).

The apostle also passes on to the new church the apostolic tradition that originated with Jesus (1 Cor. 11:2; 2 Thess. 2:15; 3:6). He unfolds the unsearchable riches of Christ, His greatness, and His all-sufficiency to the hearts of God's people (Eph. 3:8). This is what it means to build a church on Jesus Christ as the only foundation (Matt. 7:24ff.; 16:16–18; 1 Cor. 3:11; Eph. 2:20). Having the Lord Jesus Christ as the foundation means that the church learns to wholly depend upon, rest in, and live by Christ.

The gospel that the first-century apostles preached was one of Christ's lordship and God's pure and unfailing grace in Him. Paul of Tarsus, for example, did not forge people together with rules, religious duty, or legalism. Instead, he preached a gospel of grace so high and so powerful that it kicked down the gates of hell—setting the Jew free from religious duty and the Gentile free from immorality. His was a double-barreled, two-fisted gospel.

The aftermath of such ministry is that the newly founded church stood awash with the glories, the joys, and the freedom of Jesus Christ (Acts 13:52; 2 Cor. 1:24; 3:17). Note that the early apostles had been given a glorious, breathtaking revelation of Christ, which poured out of their spirits *before* they could impart that revelation to others. Consider Paul's words:

> *To reveal his Son in me, that I might preach him.*
> *(Gal. 1:16 KJV)*

The immediate and long-lasting fruit of this heavenly vision was this: God's people fell in love with their Lord and with one another.

In effect, Paul and his coworkers instructed the new Christians on how to live by the Christ who indwelt them. They showed them how to fellowship with the Lord together and individually. They equipped God's people to function corporately under the Lord's direct headship without any human officiation. The apostles also prepared the believers for the trials that they were bound to face in the future (Acts 14:22; 20:31; 1 Thess. 3:4). Consequently, the apostolic ministry was not only spiritual; it was intensely practical.[8]

After saturating the new believers with a revelation of Christ, Paul did the unthinkable. He abandoned the church into the Lord's hands. He gently pushed the believers out of their nest and left them on their own. And he did so without hiring a pastor, a clergyman, or appointing elders to supervise them. What is more, he left the church on its own in its *infancy* and in the face of imminent persecution.

According to the *Antioch Model*, the apostle typically spent anywhere from three to six months laying the ground floor of a church before leaving it. This means that Paul and his coworkers would abandon a church when it was just beginning to crawl. Elders eventually emerged within many of the assemblies and were publicly recognized. But this came later. And the elders' task was never that of governing or controlling the church. Nor was it to

---

8   Most of Paul's letters follow a similar pattern: First he deals with spiritual reality (e.g., Eph.. 1—3; Col. 1—2; Rom. 1—11), then he deals with the practical matters of church life (e.g., Eph. 4—6; Col. 3—4; Rom. 12—16).

monopolize the church's ministry. (I've discussed this in depth elsewhere.[9])

Notwithstanding, once leaving, the apostle didn't return to the church for a long period of time, anywhere from six months to two years.

This is the pattern of church planting as shown to us by Paul after he was sent out from Antioch. What a mighty, fireproof gospel Paul must have delivered to these new converts. What confidence in the risen Christ he must have had to do such a startling thing as to leave a church on its own while it was still in diapers. Roland Allen astutely observes,

> *The facts are these: St. Paul preached in a place for five or six months and then left behind him a church, not indeed free from the need of guidance, but capable of growth and expansion.... The question before us is, how he could so train his converts as to be able to leave them after so short a time with any security that they would be able to stand and grow. It seems at first sight almost incredible.... What could he have taught them in five or six months?*[10]

The net effect is that the apostle's gospel was tested to its core. If the gospel he preached was indeed Christ, or as Paul put it—if it was made of "gold, silver, and precious stones"—the church would stand through crisis (1 Cor. 3:6–15). On the other hand, if the gospel that

---

9   See my book *Reimagining Church*.
10   Roland Allen, *Missionary Methods: St. Paul's or Ours?* (Grand Rapids, MI: Eerdmans, 1962), 84–85.

the apostle brought was made of combustible materials—"wood, hay, and stubble"—it would burn to the ground when any heat came to try it.[11]

If an apostle plants the church using imperishable materials and it is nurtured properly, all it needs will spontaneously develop from within. In time, prophets, shepherds, evangelists, overseers, etc. will naturally and organically emerge—just as naturally and organically as the physical members develop on an infant as it matures. T. Austin-Sparks speaks of this experience, saying,

> *Thus, having set aside all the former system of organised Christianity, we committed ourselves to the principle of the organic. No "order" was "set up," no officers or ministries were appointed. We left it with the Lord to make manifest by "gift" and anointing who were chosen of Him for oversight and ministry. The one-man ministry has never emerged. The "overseers" have never been chosen by vote or selection, and certainly not by the expressed desire of any leader. No committees or official bodies have ever existed in any part of the work. Things in the main have issued from prayer.*[12]

Such organic development is basic to all life-forms. A rose seed has within its germ a stem, leaves, and a budding flower. If the seed is planted and properly nurtured, these features will naturally manifest

---

11   According to F. F. Bruce, this text has in view the fire of persecution as well as the fire of judgment on the last day, which will test every person's work in this life. The same concept appears in Matt. 7:24–27.

12   T. Austin-Sparks, *Explanation of the Nature and History of "This Ministry"* (Tulsa, OK: Emmanuel Church, 2004), 18.

themselves in time. In the same way, the requisite gifts and ministries of the church of Jesus Christ will naturally develop if it's planted and nurtured properly—for they are built into her very DNA.

Biblically speaking, a church is a spiritual organism, not a human organization.[13] It's a biological entity. As such, it develops naturally when the agent who planted it leaves it on its own. Of course, church planters should return periodically to water it, fertilize it, and pull up the weeds that seek to choke its life. Hence, a large part of an apostle's task is to keep foreign elements out of the church so that it can grow naturally and organically. (More on that later.)

This understanding of church development is in stark contrast to the prevalent model of trying to appoint various ministries and gifts (like elders, prophets, and teachers) on the basis of a *pro forma* adherence to a "New Testament pattern." Such a mechanical method of church formation will only produce a pathetic, paper-thin image of the church. It's like trying to create a mature rose by locating stem, leaves, and petals, then stringing them together with nylon thread. It is a violation of the organic, innate nature of the church, and it defies the biblical reality that the *ekklesia* is, in fact, a living organism.

All told, the *Antioch Model* rests on the suppositions that the church is organic, it's born by a presentation of Jesus Christ, and it organically grows in the absence of the founding apostle after he leaves it on its own. Yet it requires his return to oversee the church's growth and keep foreign elements from choking and corrupting its life (Acts 13—20). As Howard Snyder says, "Church growth is

---

13   If a church grows up to be an organization like Microsoft or General Motors, it ceases to be a church in the biblical sense of the word.

a matter of removing the hindrances to growth. The church will naturally grow if not limited by unbiblical barriers."

The *Antioch Model*, or "fresh seed planting," is the classic way in which churches were raised up in the first century. Again, Roland Allen candidly observes,

> *In a very few years, he [Paul] built the church on so firm a basis that it could live and grow in faith and in practice, that it could work out its own problems, and overcome all dangers and hindrances both from within and without.*[14]

So in the *Jerusalem Model*, the church leaves the apostolic worker. But in the *Antioch Model*, the apostolic worker leaves the church. But the end result is the same: Once the foundation of a church is laid by an apostolic worker, God's people are left on their own without any extralocal help. Comparing the *Antioch* and *Jerusalem Models*, Watchman Nee writes,

> *We find there are two ways of preaching the gospel and of establishing churches—two distinct methods illustrated respectively by Jerusalem and Antioch. From Antioch apostles go forth; from Jerusalem scattered saints go forth. In the one case, bands of apostles move out—it may be Paul and Barnabas, or Paul and Silas, or Paul and Timothy—to preach the gospel from place to place, to form churches, and to return. In the other*

---

14   Roland Allen, *Missionary Methods: St. Paul's or Ours?* (Grand Rapids, MI: Eerdmans, 1962), 7.

case, those who believe emigrate to new cities and new
lands, preaching and telling of the Lord Jesus wherever
they go; and wherever these who migrate are found,
churches spring up.[15]

The Ephesian Model

A third type of church planting began in the city of Ephesus. Therefore, we'll call it the *Ephesian Model*. In his later years, Paul traveled to Ephesus. Before he descended on that city, however, he had planted approximately eight churches over a period of seven years.

What Paul accomplished in Ephesus was as unique as it was brilliant. He made Ephesus a training center from which the gospel would go forth and where young men could be trained to plant churches. Paul rented a meeting place called the "Hall of Tyrannus" where he preached and taught every day from 11:00 a.m. to 4:00 p.m.[16] This part of the training went on for two solid years. The men who Paul trained were:

- Titus from Antioch.

- Timothy from Lystra.

- Gaius from Derbe.

---

15 Watchman Nee, *Church Affairs* (Richmond, VA: Christian Fellowship Publishers, 1982), 6–7.

16 The Western text of Acts 19:9 says that Paul used the hall from "the fifth hour to the tenth" (from 11:00 a.m. to 4:00 p.m.). F. F. Bruce points out that this reading is quite probable. See F. F. Bruce, *The Book of the Acts (Revised): New International Commentary on the New Testament* (Grand Rapids, MI: Eerdmans, 1988), 366; and F. F. Bruce, *Paul, Apostle of the Heart Set Free* (Grand Rapids, MI: Eerdmans, 2000), 290.

- Aristarchus from Thessalonica.

- Secundus from Thessalonica.

- Sopator from Berea.

- Tychicus from Ephesus.

- Trophimus from Ephesus.

Epaphras from Colosse could also be added to the list. It appears that Paul led him to the Lord while he was in Ephesus.[17] Sometime afterward, Epaphras planted three churches in the Lycus valley of Asia Minor: one in Colosse, one in Laodicea, and one in Hierapolis (Col. 1:7; 4:12–13). New Testament scholar Donald Guthrie observes,

> *It must have been during this period, for instance, that the churches at Colossae, Laodicea, and Hierapolis, all in the Lycus valley, were established, although Paul himself did not visit them. Men like Epaphras and Philemon, who were known to the apostle, possibly came under his influence in the hall of Tyrannus.*[18]

In the same vein, F. F. Bruce writes,

---

17   Epaphras seems to be the same person known as Epaphroditus. See John L. McKenzie, S. J., *Dictionary of the Bible* (New York: Macmillan, 1965), 239; *Matthew Henry's Commentary on the Whole Bible: Introduction to the Epistle to the Colossians.* Both Epaphroditus (Phil. 2:25; 4:18) and Epaphras (Philem. 23; Col. 1:7; 4:12) were coworkers with Paul, and both were with Paul during the same Roman imprisonment. Epaphras planted churches, and Paul calls Epaphroditus an *apostolos* (Phil. 2:25). This all suggests that they were one person. Further, "the name occurs very frequently in inscriptions both Greek and Latin, whether at full length Epaphroditus, or in its contracted form Epaphras" (J. B. Lightfoot, *Saint Paul's Epistle to the Philippians* [Bellingham, WA: Logos, 1913], 123).

18   Donald Guthrie, *The Apostles* (Grand Rapids, MI: Zondervan, 1975), 176.

> *To this great city, then, Paul came ... and stayed*
> *there for the best part of three years, directing the*
> *evangelization of Ephesus itself and of the province*
> *as a whole. Plainly he was assisted in this work by a*
> *number of colleagues—like Epaphras, who evangelized*
> *the Phyrgian cities of the Lycus valley (Colossae,*
> *Laodicea, and Hierapolis)—and so effectively did they*
> *work that, as Luke puts it, "all the residents of Asia*
> *heard the word of the Lord, both Jews and Greeks."*[19]

While the New Testament doesn't explicitly say that Paul trained eight men in Ephesus, it strongly suggests it. Consider the following points:

- ❧ All eight men were present in Ephesus with Paul during his lengthy season there.[20] Just as the Twelve lived with Jesus for three and a half years, so Paul's apprentices lived with Paul for about the same amount of time. In Ephesus, Paul duplicated the ministry of Jesus Christ in Galilee.

- ❧ The eight men each served as representatives from their churches to bring a financial contribution to Jerusalem. However, instead

---

19 F. F. Bruce, *Paul, Apostle of the Heart Set Free* (Grand Rapids, MI: Eerdmans, 2000), 288.

20 The following passages of Scripture put all eight men in Ephesus during the time that Paul was there: Acts 19:22; 20:4; 21:29; 1 Cor. 4:17; 16:10, 20 (Paul wrote 1 Cor. from Ephesus). One can infer that Titus was present since Luke never mentions him throughout Acts, yet we know he is present on many occasions from Paul's letters. We learn from 2 Cor. 8 that Titus represented Corinth for the Jerusalem relief fund, and it is clear from Paul's letter to Titus that Paul trained him.

of traveling directly to Jerusalem with their contribution, they met Paul in Ephesus and remained with him for three years. Timothy and Gaius were from Galatia, which is much closer to Jerusalem than was Ephesus.

- Paul spoke at the Hall of Tyrannus for five hours a day for two years. The intensity of his ministry has all the marks of training on it.

- Paul paid for his own needs and the needs of these men (Acts 20:34). Why would he support them if he wasn't training them?

- After the Ephesian trip, Paul sent these men out to work with the churches he planted as well as to plant new churches in new territories. This is similar to Jesus sending out the Twelve on their trial mission (Mark 6:7).

David Shenk and Ervin Stutzman sum up the *Ephesian Model* nicely, saying,

> *When Paul left Ephesus, he took with him a cluster of persons to visit some of the churches which he had planted in Macedonia and Greece. We may assume that these persons were leaders he had trained in Ephesus. He wanted them to see the churches he told them about in his church planting classes. These persons included*

Sopater, Aristarchus, Secundus, Gaius, Timothy, Tychicus, and Trophimus. He wanted these leaders experienced in church development in Asia also to experience Christian fellowship in European churches. This journey was a cross-cultural church planting trip for the leaders whom Paul was training.[21]

Since Paul's apprentices were from different churches in diverse regions (Galatia, Macedonia, Achaia, and Asia), they undoubtedly learned from one another as each man shared his unique experience of organic church life in his own culture. Later in the Ephesian training, Paul sent his eight apprentices all over Asia Minor to preach the gospel of Christ and plant new churches. Some of these churches are listed in Revelation 2 and 3. F. F. Bruce writes,

While Paul stayed in Ephesus, a number of his colleagues carried out missionary activity in neighboring cities. During those years his colleague Epaphras appears to have evangelized the cities of the Lycus valley, Colossae, Laodicea, and Hierapolis—cities which Paul evidently did not visit in person (Colossians 1:7–8; 2:1; 4:12–13). Perhaps all seven of the churches in Asia addressed in the Revelation of John were also founded about this time. The province was intensely evangelized, and remained one of the leading centers of Christianity for many centuries.[22]

---

21   David Shenk and Ervin Stutzman, *Creating Communities of the Kingdom* (Scottdale, PA: Herald, 1988), 154.

22   F. F. Bruce, *The Book of the Acts (Revised): New International Commentary on the New Testament* (Grand Rapids, MI: Eerdmans, 1988), 366.

In short, Paul's eight apprentices were the equivalent of the Lord's twelve apostles. The Twelve brought the gospel to the Jewish world; Paul's young coworkers brought it to the Gentile world.

The Roman Model

The fourth and final model is illustrated by the church in Rome. I call it "inverted transplantation." In the *Jerusalem Model,* one church transplants itself into many different cities, thus creating many new churches. But in the *Roman Model,* Christians living in many different churches transplant themselves into one city to found one new church. This is what appears to have happened in Rome, Italy.

The evidence for this model is compelling. Some New Testament scholars have argued that Romans 16 was not written to the church in Rome but to the church in Ephesus. The reason? Paul had never been to Rome before he wrote Romans. Yet he knew all the people listed in chapter 16, some of whom had previously lived in Ephesus.

Others have argued that the people Paul greets in Romans 16 coincidentally moved to Rome, and they all ended up in the same church. But these two theories are unlikely.

It seems that the original Roman church was primarily Jewish. Luke tells us that visitors from Rome came to Jerusalem on the day of Pentecost and heard Peter preach the gospel (Acts 2:10). It appears that some of them returned to Rome and began to gather there. Priscilla and Aquila were probably part of this group. However, in AD 49, Emperor Claudius passed an edict that expelled all Jews from Rome (Acts 18:2).

When Paul writes his letter to the Romans in AD 57, many Jewish believers are back in the church. Many Gentile believers are in it also. In Romans 16, Paul greets twenty-six individuals and five households, all of whom he knows personally. Virtually all of them have come from the various churches that Paul planted over the years.

The scenario that best fits the evidence is that Paul sent Priscilla and Aquila back to Rome once Claudius's edict was lifted in AD 54. One clue that supports this view is how Priscilla and Aquila helped Paul plant the church in Ephesus. Four years before Paul wrote his famous Roman letter, he brought this remarkable couple to Ephesus and left them there to labor before he returned to plant the Ephesian church (Acts 18:18–19). New Testament scholars William Sanday and Arthur Headlam observe,

> *That Prisca and Aquila should be at Rome is just what we might expect from one with so keen an eye for the strategy of a situation as St. Paul. When he was himself established and in full work at Ephesus with the intention of visiting Rome, it would at once occur to him what valuable work they might be doing there and what an excellent preparation they might make for his own visit, while in his immediate surroundings they were almost superfluous. So that instead of presenting any difficulty, that he should send them back to Rome where they were already known, is most natural.*[23]

---

23 William Sanday and Arthur Headlam, *A Critical and Exegetical Commentary on the Epistle to the Romans* (New York: Charles Scribner's Sons, 1905), xxvii.

After sending Priscilla and Aquila ahead of him to Rome, Paul asked various individuals, both Jew and Gentile, from the various churches he planted to move to Rome.[24] The goal? To plant a multicultural church of Jew and Gentile in the cosmopolitan city of Rome.[25]

Paul planned to preach the gospel in Rome and use this newly transplanted church as a platform to reach the city. (He eventually came to Rome, but not in a way that he expected. He arrived there as a prisoner.) The church in Rome turned out to be a glorious church—the envy of the empire.[26]

This reconstruction fits the evidence much better than to assume that Romans 16 is part of the Ephesian letter and was misplaced with the letter to the Romans. There is no strong textual or manuscript evidence that would warrant us to separate Romans 16 from the Roman epistle.[27] It's also more reasonable than to assume that the twenty-six individuals coincidentally relocated to Rome in the space of only three years.[28]

Further, in Romans 15:20, Paul makes plain that he will not build a church on another person's foundation.[29] And he talks to the

24 He also asked some of his Jewish kinfolk from Jerusalem to relocate to Rome (Rom. 16:7).

25 Other scholars like Peter Lampe have also suggested that Priscilla and Aquila went back to Rome to get a church started and to prepare for Paul's visit there. "The Roman Christians of Romans 16," in *The Romans Debate*, ed. K.P. Donfriend, 2nd ed. (Peabody, MA: Hendrickson, 1991), 220.

26 Tragically, many (if not all) of the believers in Rome were martyred during Nero's slaughter of the Christians in AD 65.

27 Douglas Moo successfully refutes the idea that Romans 16 is not part of the Roman letter in his *Epistle to the Romans: New International Commentary of the New Testament* (Grand Rapids, MI: Eerdmans, 1996), 5–9.

28 Priscilla and Aquila moved to Rome sometime after the spring of AD 54, when Claudius's ban was lifted. The letter to the Romans was written in the winter of AD 57.

29 Douglas Moo says that the church in Rome was not planted or visited by any other apostle before Paul wrote his letter (*Epistle to the Romans*, 897). F. F. Bruce says that this text is not in direct reference to the Roman church (*Romans: Tyndale New Testament Commentaries* [Grand Rapids, MI: Eerdmans, 1985], 248). And Ben Witherington says, "Nothing we find in Romans suggests that the Christian community there has an apostolic foundation, much less a Peterine apostolic foundation" (*Paul's Letter to the Romans: A Socio-Rhetorical Commentary* [Grand Rapids, MI: Eerdmans, 2004], 354).

Romans as if he were their apostle. In Romans 1:15, Paul says that he will preach the gospel in Rome when he arrives in the city. Several scholars working in the field of epistolography have concluded that Paul sent his greetings in Romans 16 in order to make evident the nature of his relationship with the believers in Rome and thus establish his apostolic authority there.[30]

Piecing all the evidence together, then, it's reasonable to believe that Paul is the apostle in Rome by inverted transplantation. This scenario explains how Paul could know all the people he greets in Romans 16 without disconnecting it from the Roman letter. It also gives us clear insight into yet another way of planting the church of Jesus Christ.

The Team Concept

The New Testament clearly demonstrates that God is a fan of apostolic workers laboring in teams, particularly in pairs. This is not *always* the case throughout Scripture, for Paul, Peter, Timothy, Titus, Epaphras, et al. labored in some places alone.[31] However, the general rule is that the work of God was accomplished by those who labored together.[32] Note the following:

✤ The twelve apostles are listed in pairs (Matt. 10:2–4).

---

30 See L. Ann Jervis's *The Purpose of Romans*; and Harry Gamble's *The Textual History of the Letter to the Romans*.

31 Acts 9:32ff.; 1 Thess. 3:2, 5; Col. 4:12–13; Titus 3:12; 2 Tim. 4:20.

32 This does not imply that one of the workers was not in the "lead" when they traveled together. Paul, for instance, was the "chief speaker" when he and Barnabas labored together in Lystra (Acts 14:12).

- Jesus sent the Twelve out in pairs for a trial mission (Mark 6:7).

- Jesus sent the seventy-two out in pairs for a field assignment (Luke 10:1).

- The Twelve (minus Judas) are listed in pairs when Luke mentions them in the upper room (Acts 1:13).

- The Lord often sent a pair of His disciples to fulfill some task (Matt. 21:1; Luke 22:8).

- Peter and John worked together as a pair (Acts 3:1ff.; 4:1, 13ff.; 8:14ff.).

- Paul and Barnabas worked together as a pair (Acts 13—15:35).

- Barnabas and Mark worked together as a pair (Acts 15:39).

- Paul and Silas worked together as a pair (Acts 15:40).

- Paul sent pairs of men to serve in the work (Acts 19:22; 2 Cor. 8:16–18).

The above examples should not be misconstrued to be an artificial or mechanical method. Instead, the workers who traveled together grew up in organic church life with one another (Luke 22:8; John

20:2–3; and Acts 3:1). Traveling together was simply the natural impulse of spiritual life.

The team concept reflects the need for Christian workers to have peers. This prevents them from being self-styled lone rangers in God's work. Although team ministry is a clear biblical pattern, we rarely see it in our day. I personally consider this to be one of the great shames and indictments of our age. While it may not always be possible or practical in every context, it should happen more than it does.

Strategy for Spontaneous Expansion

There's another point worth mentioning that has to do with Paul's church-planting strategy.[33] Paul was an urban church planter. For the most part, he bypassed the rural areas and ignored the small communities.[34] Instead, he went directly to the major urban areas. He concentrated on planting indigenous churches in influential cities that had large populations.

It is for this reason that the word *pagan* has come to refer to non-Christian people. The word *pagan* is derived from the ancient word for *farmer*, which means country-dweller. (A similar etymology lies behind the word *heathen*. The heathens were those who lived on the "heath," i.e., out in the country.)

---

33 The exact strategy that the apostles used in their preaching to the lost is beyond the scope of this book. However, there were two major venues for it: the principle of the marketplace (Acts 17:17), where the gospel is preached to a heathen audience, and the principle of the synagogue (Acts 17:1–3), where the gospel is preached to a religious audience. While Paul's calling was primarily to the Gentile (Gal. 2:7–9), he preached to the Jew first (Rom. 1:16). Conversely, while Peter's calling was primarily to the Jew (Gal. 2:7–9), he preached to the Gentile as well (Acts 10:1ff.). There was, therefore, considerable overlap between the callings of the two men. Further, both men labored in Judea, Antioch, Corinth, Rome, Galatia, and Asia.

34 The exceptions are found in Derbe (a small town) and the surrounding regions around Lycaonia (Acts 14:6).

Christianity was rarely successful outside the cities of the ancient world. Because our faith is inherently relational, the church was unable to successfully take root outside of urban settings. In urban areas, Christians could see one another in their day-to-day lives and easily care for one another. In the countryside, believers were more isolated from each other. Therefore, they had a difficult time fleshing out the "one anothers" that the New Testament so often emphasizes. Consequently, Christianity has always been dominantly urban.

But Paul's strategy in planting churches in large cities went beyond making it conducive for community life. It was also to allow the gospel to spread spontaneously (1 Thess. 1:8). An organic church, when properly functioning, will draw the lost by her sheer magnetism and charm. In the big city, where there's no shortage of people who live in close proximity, this is feasible. But in the countryside, it's far more difficult. Speaking of the "spontaneous expansion of the church," Roland Allen writes,

> *This then is what I mean by spontaneous expansion. I mean the expansion which follows the unexhorted and unorganized activity of individual members of the church explaining to others the gospel which they have found for themselves; I mean the expansion which follows the irresistible attraction of the Christian church for men who see its ordered life, and are drawn to it by desire to discover the secret of a life which they instinctively desire to share; I mean also the expansion of the church by the addition of new churches.*[35]

35   Roland Allen, *The Spontaneous Expansion of the Church* (Grand Rapids, MI: Eerdmans, 1962), 7.

Pisidian Antioch, Philippi, Thessalonica, Corinth, Ephesus, and Rome were not sleepy little towns. They were strategic cities where spontaneous expansion could easily occur. On this score, F. F. Bruce remarks,

> *So Paul traveled along the Roman highways, the main lines of communication, preaching the gospel and planting churches in strategic centres. From those centres the saving message would be disseminated.*[36]

Strikingly, to Paul's mind an entire province was evangelized if he planted a few churches in the central cities that belonged to it. When Paul wrote his letter to the Romans, he and his coworkers had planted fewer than twenty churches in Galatia, Greece, Asia Minor, and Rome. Yet according to Paul, the gospel had been "fully preached" from Jerusalem all the way to Rome.

In only ten years—with fewer than twenty Gentile churches on the planet—Paul felt that there was no further place for him to preach in the regions from Jerusalem to Rome (Rom. 15:19–24 KJV). As Donald Guthrie puts it,

> *Turning to his immediate plans, he [Paul] makes the astonishing statement that he finds no further room for work in the regions just mentioned. This does not mean that the areas have been completely evangelized, for Paul's strategy was to plant churches in important centers and then to expect the developing churches to*

---

36 F. F. Bruce, *Paul, Apostle of the Heart Set Free* (Grand Rapids, MI: Eerdmans, 2000), 315.

> *evangelize the surrounding district. Only by this means*
> *was he able to work in so many areas.*[37]

Church-planting strategy and the guidance of the Holy Spirit are
not mutually exclusive. Because apostolic workers are sent by God,[38]
the work they do belongs to God and not to them. Accordingly, the
Lord orchestrates and pioneers His own work. He chooses where
the gospel is to be preached and where His workers are to travel. He
also engineers the timing when this should take place (Acts 10:9–11,
19–20; 13:2–4; 16:6–8; 18:8–11; 23:11; Gal. 2:2).

Apostles work in areas where a local church invites them or
if they have received a revelation to go to a particular place. First-
century workers were not strangers to the Lord's inward guidance
(1 Cor. 2:7–16). After all, it is Jesus Christ who creates the church by
His Spirit. Humans are but His instruments.

Summary

To recap, the New Testament gives us four ways in which churches
were planted in the first century and visible communities of God's
kingdom were established. They are:

> ❧ *The Jerusalem Model*—A group of apostolic
> workers spends years raising up one large
> church. After a number of years, the church
> is transplanted into many different cities, thus

---

37 Donald Guthrie, *The Apostles* (Grand Rapids, MI: Zondervan, 1975), 256.

38 God is the One who sends workers (John 20:21; Acts 13:2; 1 Cor. 1:17). However, divine sending is
typically manifested through a church, the representatives of a church, or by an older worker.

creating many new churches. The workers visit those new churches and lay fresh foundations for them.

- *The Antioch Model*—Apostolic workers are sent out from a local church to plant new churches in new cities. The workers leave those churches in their infancy but give periodic help and encouragement as they mature.

- *The Ephesian Model*—An older worker resides in a particular city to plant a new church and train younger workers. He then sends those workers out to plant new churches in nearby regions.

- *The Roman Model*—Christians from many different churches transplant themselves into a particular city to establish one new church.

Because these four models of church planting are God-given, I don't believe they can be improved upon. Ironically, it is rare to find many people observing them today. Along this line, Watchman Nee writes,

> *Though today the places we visit and the conditions we meet may be vastly different from those of the Scripture record, yet in principle the experience of the first apostles may well serve as our example.... Christianity has lost*

its original purity, and everything connected with it is in a false and confused state. Despite that fact, our work today is still the same as in the days of the early apostles—to found and build up local churches, the local expressions of the Body of Christ.[39]

Roland Allen echoes the same sentiment, saying,

Today if a man ventures to suggest that there may be something in the methods by which St. Paul attained such wonderful results worthy of our careful attention, and perhaps of our imitation, he is in danger of being accused of revolutionary tendencies.... All I can say is, "This is the way of Christ and His apostles." If any man answers, "That is out of date," or "Times have changed" ... I can only repeat, "This is the way of Christ and His apostles," and leave him to face that issue.[40]

I wish that every person who feels called to plant churches would reexamine the principles of the New Testament and, with the Lord's leading, reclaim them.

---

39 Watchman Nee, *The Normal Christian Church Life* (Anaheim, CA: Living Stream Ministry, 1980), 133.

40 Roland Allen, *Missionary Methods: St. Paul's or Ours?* (Grand Rapids, MI: Eerdmans, 1962), 2–4.

CHAPTER 2

RESTORING THE ITINERANT WORKER

> *No solution, no matter how creative or highpowered,*
> *can succeed if you have defined the problem incorrectly.*
> *Put differently: more important than giving the*
> *right answers is asking the right questions.... Simply*
> *changing the materials, programs, and activities is not*
> *enough. We must change how we perceive the church,*
> *how we see God expressing Himself in the world*
> *through the church, and how we do church.*

—William A. Beckham

In our last chapter, we explored the four ways in which churches were planted in the first century. All of them are hardly known today. While much is said these days about "equipping the saints for the work of the ministry," there is often very little fleshing out of this principle in real life. The litmus test of such equipping is if the leader

could leave a local congregation on its own without any official
leadership in place and it's capable of functioning in his absence. This
is precisely what Paul of Tarsus did again and again with the churches
he planted. By doing so, his gospel and his efforts to "equip" God's
people were put to the test.

This brings us to a critical question. What are the scriptural
ingredients for planting organic churches?

The Worker and the Work

Virtually every church in the first century was given birth at the
hands of an extralocal, itinerant worker who eventually left it on its
own. (Note: The few churches mentioned in the New Testament that
emerged without the direct aid of an itinerant worker were virtually
always helped and encouraged by one after its birth.)

This person is known by the following names: "apostle," "sent one,"
"worker," "foundation layer," "church planter," et al. Again, an apostle is
someone who establishes churches. As William S. McBirnie says,

> *Having traced their lives very carefully, from every
> scholarly source obtainable, this writer has concluded
> that without exception the one thing the apostles did
> was to build churches—not buildings of course, but
> congregations. As far as the record reveals, the apostles
> established a congregation.*[1]

The term *worker* is particularly favorable. Jesus used it in His
messages (Matt. 9:37–38; 20:1–2; Luke 10:2, 7). Paul used it in his

1   William Steuart McBirnie, *The Search for the Twelve Apostles* (Carol Stream, IL: Tyndale, 1973), 27–28.

letters (1 Cor. 3:9; 2 Cor. 6:1; 11:13; Col. 4:11). And Luke refers to the ministry of planting and nurturing local churches as "the work":

> *While they were worshiping the Lord and fasting, the Holy Spirit said, "Set apart for me Barnabas and Saul for the work to which I have called them." (Acts 13:2)*

> *From Attalia they sailed back to Antioch, where they had been committed to the grace of God for the work they had now completed. (Acts 14:26)*

> *But Paul did not think it wise to take him, because he had deserted them in Pamphylia and had not continued with them in the work. (Acts 15:38)*

In discussing the careful distinction between the "the work" and "the church," New Testament scholar Robert Banks writes,

> *These two, the church and the work, should never be confused, as they generally have been in subsequent Christian thinking. Paul views his missionary operation not as an "ekklesia" but rather as something existing independently alongside the scattered Christian communities.... Its [the work's] purpose is first the preaching of the gospel and the founding of churches, and then the provision of assistance so that they may reach maturity.*[2]

---

2   Robert Banks, *Paul's Idea of Community* (Peabody, MA: Hendrickson, 1994), 168–69.

Watchman Nee adds,

> *In the will of God, "the church" and "the work" follow*
> *two distinct lines. The work belongs to the apostles, while*
> *the churches belong to the local believers. The apostles*
> *are responsible for the work in any place, and the church*
> *is responsible for all the children of God there.*[3]

We will discuss the difference between the work and the church
in a later chapter, as it's a critical issue.

Stewards of the Mystery

According to Scripture, an apostle is a "sent one." He is a messenger.
He's an envoy *sent* to declare—to preach—a message, and to be a living
witness to that message. And out of that message, a spiritual community
is raised up by the Holy Spirit. Note the following passages:

> *And he ordained twelve, that they should be with him,*
> *and that he might send them forth to preach. (Mark*
> *3:14 KJV)*

> *For Christ did not send me to baptize, but to preach*
> *the gospel. (1 Cor. 1:17)*

> *And how shall they preach, except they be sent? As it*
> *is written, How beautiful are the feet of them that*

preach the gospel of peace, and bring glad tidings of
good things! (Rom. 10:15 KJV)[4]

Because first-century workers were sent, they were itinerant.
That is, they traveled. They were pioneers and explorers mostly on
the move.[5] But that's not all. Christian workers held in their hands
a stewardship. That stewardship was to articulate the mystery of
God to His people (1 Cor. 4:1ff.). The "mystery," as Paul called it,
is the consuming revelation of God's eternal purpose in Christ that
burns in the hearts of all who have been genuinely sent.[6]

One of the worker's main tasks was to impart this revelation—or
vision—to the Lord's people. As Proverbs says, "Where there is no
prophetic vision the people cast off restraint" (29:18 ESV). Without
a unified vision of the Lord and His ageless purpose, God's people
disintegrate—they run amok—they fall apart. Without an internal
"seeing" of Jesus Christ, they lose heart, motivation, purpose, and
harmony.

A shared vision of Christ and of God's purpose in Him has
sustaining power. It also produces unity. Such vision of the Lord
is the only proper foundation upon which a church can be built.

One of the principal tasks of the Christian worker, then,
was to preach to God's people the unsearchable riches of Christ
beyond telling (Eph. 3:8). First-century workers had a matchless

---

4   See also Acts 14:7, 21; 16:9–10; 20:24; Rom. 1:1, 9, 15–16; 2:16; 15:16, 19–20, 29; 16:25; 1 Cor.
4:15; 9:12, 16–18, 23; 15:1; 2 Cor. 2:12; 4:3–4; 10:14, 16; 11:7; Gal. 1:11; 2:2, 5, 7, 14; 4:13; Eph. 1:13;
3:6; 6:19; Phil. 1:5, 7, 12, 17, 27; Col. 1:5, 23; 1 Thess. 1:5; 2:2, 4, 8–9; 3:2; 2 Thess. 2:14; 1 Tim. 1:11;
2 Tim. 1:8.

5   While they sometimes took up temporary residence in various places, they consistently traveled and
were mainly on the move.

6   For a detailed discussion of the mystery of God's eternal purpose, see my book *From Eternity to Here.*

revelation of Jesus Christ and the mystery of God's eternal purpose in Him. And they were able to articulate that purpose so that the Lord's people would be arrested by it. This was a major mark of Paul's ministry of planting churches. Consider the following passages:

> *Unto me, who am less than the least of all saints, is this grace given, that I should preach among the Gentiles the unsearchable riches of Christ; and to make all men see what is the fellowship of the mystery, which from the beginning of the world hath been hid in God, who created all things by Jesus Christ. (Eph. 3:8–9 KJV)*

> *And for me, that utterance may be given unto me, that I may open my mouth boldly, to make known the mystery of the gospel. (Eph. 6:19 KJV)*

> *Praying also for us, that God would open unto us a door of utterance, to speak the mystery of Christ, for which I am also in bonds. (Col. 4:3 KJV; see also Rom. 16:25; 1 Cor. 2:7; Eph. 1:9; Col. 1:26; 2:2)*

Spiritual Equippers

One of the key roles of first-century Christian workers was to equip God's people to minister Christ to one another. R. Paul Stevens throws light on the phrase "to equip the saints" when he says,

> *The Greek word for equipping, "katartismos," is used
> as a noun only once—in Ephesians 4:12. But the word
> has an interesting medical history in classical Greek.
> To equip is to put a bone or a part of the human body
> into right relationship with the other parts of the body
> so that every part fits thoroughly.... A Greek doctor
> would "equip" a body by putting a bone back into
> its correct relationship with the other members of the
> body.[7]*

How exactly did apostolic workers equip the saints? How did they coordinate the various parts of the body of Christ so that each was empowered to function? Aside from supplying the church with a deep and profound presentation of Jesus Christ, there were a number of other ingredients involved. The following six are most important:

(1) REMOVING THE SIN CONSCIOUSNESS

Organic churches have open-participatory meetings where each member shares something of the Lord with the rest of church. But one of the major obstacles that hinders believers from functioning in such meetings is the consciousness of sin. This is the sense of guilt. The sense of condemnation. The sense of unworthiness.

In the first century, the Christian worker's task was to empower God's people by setting them free from guilt. The worker did so by showing God's people that they are blameless in God's eyes. He showed them how God sees them in Christ, and that Christ's shed

---

7   R. Paul Stevens, *Liberating the Laity* (Vancouver, Canada: Regent, 2002), 25.

blood was enough to satisfy God's demands. He also provoked them to repent when necessary.

By preaching a gospel of unfailing grace, void of legalism, first-century workers armed God's people with a clean conscience—free from the consciousness of sin. This empowered the early Christians to open their mouths and boldly share the Lord with one another (Heb. 9:14; 10:1–25) as well as to the lost.

(2) PROVIDING PRACTICAL TOOLS

The first-century Christian worker's message was Christ. Yet as he declared the glory of God in the face of Jesus Christ, the worker had a responsibility to show God's people *how* to experience the Lord's glory by simple, doable means.

This element is vital because an organic church cannot be sustained unless the members are experiencing an ongoing, personal relationship with Christ. Herein lies one of the most important tasks of a Christian worker. He himself must have a fresh, living, ongoing, personal relationship with his Lord along with a knowledge of how to pass it on to others.

Point: Unless God's people are awakened to an indwelling Lord, they will never be able to sustain organic church life.

This brings us to the issue of leadership. A good definition of a leader is someone who knows the next step. This "knowing" is based on "seeing." Moses could not build the tabernacle without first following God and being shown the pattern from above. In the same way, first-century workers had great insight into God's ageless purpose. They possessed spiritual sight—the ability to see the unseen.

Paul, the model Christian worker, calls himself a "master builder" (1 Cor. 3:10 NASB). The Greek word translated "master builder" is *architekton*, from which our word *architect* is derived. This word refers to the spiritual gift that gives one the capacity to see how the different parts of God's spiritual building fit together with the other parts.

An architect has the insight to see where the stairway fits into the living room, where the master bathroom will be located, how the plumbing should be laid out, where and when the electrical outlets should be installed, etc. It's the same with those who build God's spiritual house. As Melvin Hodges says,

> *The church planter will be a man of vision. He will see possibilities where others only see obstacles. He will be highly motivated and persevere in spite of discouraging set-backs. His vision is backed up by a solid faith that God has sent him to do this work and will see him through. Most churches are established because of the vision, spiritual burden, sacrifice, and perseverance of some individual who gave himself to the task of church planting.*[8]

In a word, first-century workers were those who followed the Lord wholeheartedly, saw the next step, and had the ability to show God's people how to take it. They were gifted not only in imparting vision, but also in catalyzing others to work together toward fulfilling it.

---

8   Melvin L. Hodges, *A Guide to Church Planting* (Chicago: Moody, 1973), 30–31.

(3) INSTILLING CONFIDENCE IN SPIRITUAL GIFTINGS

Without confidence, the people of God will stay muted and passive. Throughout Paul's letters, he reiterates again and again the confidence that he had in the believers and in their abilities (Gal. 5:10; 2 Thess. 3:4; 2 Cor. 2:3; 7:16; 8:22; Rom. 15:14; Phil. 1:6).

First-century workers demonstrated confidence in God's work in the church. Instilling such confidence in the Lord's people helped empower them to function and serve. It's the same way with Christian workers today. They are confident in the Holy Spirit and in God's people—all of whom are anointed by the Spirit.

(4) MODELING BY EXAMPLE

As vital as the above ministry is to church formation, the *example* that a Christian worker sets before God's people is of great importance. A church is equipped not only by preaching, but also by modeling. First-century workers modeled what they preached by their own example. Paul often makes mention of this aspect in his letters:

> *Join with others in following my example, brothers, and take note of those who live according to the pattern we gave you. (Phil. 3:17)*

> *Because our gospel came to you not simply with words, but also with power, with the Holy Spirit and with deep conviction. You know how we lived among you for your sake. You became imitators of us and of the Lord; in spite of severe suffering, you welcomed*

*the message with the joy given by the Holy Spirit.
(1 Thess. 1:5–6)*

*For you yourselves know how you ought to follow our
example. We were not idle when we were with you.
(2 Thess. 3:7)*

*In everything set them an example by doing what
is good. In your teaching show integrity, seriousness.
(Titus 2:7)*

*Follow my example, as I follow the example of Christ.
(1 Cor. 11:1)*

Obviously, this doesn't mean that workers are perfect and free
from making mistakes. Peter is the summary witness that apostles
are fallen people who make mistakes—sometimes very big ones.[9] It
rather has to do with their character, which is evidenced by their
consistent patterns of behavior.

From reading Paul's letters carefully, we get the distinct impression
that Paul modeled how the church was to take care of its members
and love the lost. He modeled how the members were to fellowship
with the Lord and pray for one another. He modeled how they were
to handle problems, worship, and live by the Lord's indwelling life.

---

9   Peter obstructed the Lord's plans on numerous occasions, he disowned Jesus three times, and he
yielded to human pressure when the truth was at stake (John 18:10; Luke 22:51; Matt. 16:22; 26:69ff.; Gal.
2:11ff.). Yet the New Testament consistently regards him as a great apostle (Mark 16:7; John 21:15ff.; Acts
1—12; 1 Cor. 15:5).

It's not enough to simply teach and preach these things; modeling them before God's people is just as critical.

(5) REMOVING FOREIGN ELEMENTS

Another way that workers help God's people to function is by *preventing* foreign elements from entering into the church to choke its life and distort its natural features. Perhaps an illustration will help explain this aspect.

An admirer once asked Michelangelo how he sculpted the famous statue of David that now sits in Florence, Italy. Michelangelo responded by offering this simple explanation: "I first fixed my attention on the slab of raw marble. I studied it, and then I chipped away all that wasn't David."

Michelangelo's description can be applied to how apostolic workers plant and sustain churches. *One of the major goals of those who plant churches is to remove everything that isn't Jesus Christ.* Apostolic workers not only built a rock-solid foundation of Christ, but they were also careful to remove everything that was not Christ.

(6) DEFYING ENTROPY

One thing that will kill the functioning of the body of Christ is entropy. Entropy is the natural breakdown and disintegration that occurs in all life-forms. Things that are left to themselves tend toward entropy. But entropy not only applies to physical life systems; it also applies to Christian community.

In time, entropy degrades every human enterprise. We all run out of steam over time. The persistent energy that is required to

RESTORING THE ITINERANT WORKER   63

keep a group of Christians moving forward without an institutional structure can be quite taxing.

When entropy sets into an organic church, the type A personalities begin to fill the vacuum. This is the pattern of church history. Because of the powerful force of entropy, the early church moved from an organic, shared-life community to a hierarchal, one up/one down, top-heavy organization.

First-century workers withstood the inevitable force of entropy. They recentered and reenergized the church toward Christ and gave it fresh direction. This is yet another way in which church planters equip God's people to function and keep the church afloat.

How God Produces Apostolic Workers

Perhaps one of the least understood principles of the work of God today is that itinerant workers always emerged from the soil of an existing church. They were people who were given a unique revelation of Christ and of God's eternal purpose in Him. They were well acquainted with the mystery of God. And they were specially equipped to articulate that mystery to others (Eph. 1:9; 3:2–11; Col. 1:24–29). But beyond all this, a Christian worker learned all of these spiritual realities in the context of an existing organic church where he was a nonleader.[10]

In fact, a large part of a worker's preparation for service is to live in the context of an organic church *before* he is sent out. It is within this rare setting that the Christian worker both experiences and learns the spiritual and practical realities of body life.

---

10   Such a person may be raised up by God to be an elder in an organic church before he is sent out to the work, but that will not be immediate. Paul and Barnabas were prophets and/or teachers in the church in Antioch before they were sent out from that church to labor apostolically (Acts 13:1–2).

Consequently, first-century workers didn't leave the synagogue on Saturday and start planting churches on Sunday. *They first experienced that which they were sent out to begin.* This principle is critical. And aspiring "church planters" who have never lived a day in the context of an authentic organic church should take serious heed to it.

A seminary education cannot equip a person to raise up the church of the living God—nor can any position in an institutional church or Bible study group. Only time spent in an organic expression of the body of Christ can equip a person for such work.

To frame it another way, you cannot produce that which you have never experienced. What is more, the gore and glory—the testing and transforming—the sifting and soaring—the brokenness and beautifying—the exposure and enlargement that organic church life affords are vital for preparing those who are called to God's work.

Thus, to blithely launch out to plant an organic church without such preparation is sheer folly. And it reflects a profound misunderstanding of God's ways. The exacting nature of body life is designed to prevent would-be workers from becoming clergy-on-wheels who lord over the Lord's people like distant bosses. Living in organic church life as a nonleader is designed to produce brokenness and humility. It's designed to make workers safe to God's people. (One of the major marks of spiritual safety is that workers have peers.) It's also designed to equip them so they know what they are doing in raising up the house of God. Put differently, in God's work, it is not only the method that's important. The person is just as critical. As Watchman Nee says,

> *We must realize clearly that even though we adopt*
> *apostolic methods, unless we have apostolic consecration,*

apostolic faith and apostolic power, we shall still fail
to see apostolic results. We dare not underestimate
the value of apostolic methods—they are absolutely
essential if we are to have apostolic fruits—but we
must not overlook the need of apostolic spirituality,
and we must not fear apostolic persecution.[11]

Helpers in the Work

The New Testament is crystal clear that not all Christians are called
to apostolic ministry (1 Cor. 12:28ff.). However, many are called and
gifted to *assist* in the apostolic work. We have already seen that Paul
had a number of "coworkers" who also planted churches. Yet in
addition to these coapostles, Paul had a group of men and women
who assisted him in his work.[12]

Some were undoubtedly prophets and teachers; others may not
have been. But all of them had a heart for the Lord's work and were
willing to serve in whatever capacity they could. Among them were:
John Mark, Onesiphorus, Sosthenes, Erastus, Urbanus, Priscilla and
Aquila, Crescens, Onesimus, Philemon, Archippus, and Phoebe.

In addition, Peter and Paul often had a supporting team to
accommodate them on their trips (Acts 10:23; 11:12; 12:25; 15:2).
Unfortunately, some Christians have the misguided idea that being

---

11   Watchman Nee, *The Normal Christian Church Life* (Anaheim, CA: Living Stream Ministry, 1980), 36.

12   There were other men and women whom Paul regarded as "workers," "coworkers," and "fellow-
workers." These people were in addition to the men Paul trained in Ephesus. Among them were: Apollos,
Barnabas, Silas, Demas, Jesus called Justus, Tryphena, Tryphosa, Persis, Artemas, Clement, Euodia, Syntyche,
Andronicus, and Junia. For details, see the following articles in *Dictionary of Paul and His Letters* (Downers
Grove, IL: InterVarsity, 1993): "Church Order and Government," 136–37; and "Paul and His Coworkers,"
183–89.

a church planter is the "end-all-be-all" of being a Christian. Such a romanticized notion of being a Christian worker is both tragic and foolish.

Just because some people are not called to plant churches does not mean that they are second-class Christians. Hardly. As stated above, the people who assisted Paul had a heart for God's work and were very much involved with it. In fact, the work could not have advanced without them.

The truth is that there are many gifts in the body of Christ beyond that of apostles that are just as valuable to the Lord: Prophets, teachers, evangelists, helpers, exhorters, and those who show mercy are just a few of them (Eph. 4:11ff.; 1 Cor. 12:28ff.; Rom. 12:4ff.).

In the traditional church system, those who feel "called" of God are given three main options for ministry. You prepare to be either a pastor, a missionary, or a worship leader. But this restricted view of ministry is not biblical. And I believe it unwittingly forces many "called" Christians into a job description that God never intended.

In the same way, the New Testament doesn't support the idea that there are church planters and then the rest of the body of Christ. Not at all. There are many different giftings and ministries, which all work together to produce and build up the church of the living God.

A Challenge to All Church Planters

Perhaps some of you believe that apostles no longer exist. Without a doubt, the twelve apostles hold a unique place in God's economy (Luke 22:30; Rev. 21:14).[13]

---

13   The Twelve would include Matthias, who replaced Judas Iscariot (Acts 1:26).

Yet Scripture mentions other apostles beyond the Twelve. Paul and Barnabas (Acts 14:4, 14; 1 Cor. 9:1–6); James, the Lord's brother (Gal. 1:19); and Timothy and Silas (1 Thess. 1:1; 2:6) are just some of the apostles who appear throughout the pages of the New Testament. Apostolic *ministry,* therefore, continued beyond the death of the original Twelve. It did not pass away after the first century. Neither was it transmitted formally through an institutional hierarchy.

While apostles are not writing Scripture today, they are still divinely commissioned to build the body of Christ (1 Cor. 12:28–29; Eph. 4:11). The chief work of an apostle is to raise up churches. This does not mean that a church cannot be birthed without the hand of an apostle. The churches of Syrian Antioch, Caesarea, Tyre, and Ptolemais do not appear to have been founded by one.

But all of these churches received help from an apostolic worker shortly after their births. Again, *every church in the New Testament was either planted or greatly helped by an apostolic worker.*

Apostolic workers aren't called to establish missions, denominations, cell groups, parachurch organizations, or institutional "churches." They are called to plant *ekklesias* that are grounded and sustained by Jesus Christ—the Chief Architect of the church (1 Cor. 3:6–15).

Whether you believe that apostles exist today or not, there's no doubt that there are those who are still gifted to plant, equip, and nurture Christian communities. So if you don't like the word *apostle,* simply replace it with *church planter* or *itinerant worker.*

I'm convinced that Paul of Tarsus best modeled how the church of the living God should be planted. I see no evidence that the way he raised up churches was tied to his culture. As we will see in the next chapter, I believe it was tied to the unchanging nature of God Himself.

It happened like this: An apostolic team walks into a town. They are willing to be spit on, stomped on, buried, and burned. They endure the worst conditions known to humanity (2 Cor. 11:23ff.; 6:4–10; Acts 13—25). But as long as they have breath in their lungs, they continue to preach the gospel of Jesus Christ and raise up God's house.

What's motivating them in the face of such odds? They have been given a large dose of Jesus Christ. They have been overwhelmed by a vision of Christ and of God's ultimate passion for a bride, a building, a body, and a family. That vision burns in them. It consumes their very lives. In everything they do, the love of Christ compels them (2 Cor. 5:14).

The apostles lead some people to the Lord. They call men and women to repent, to believe the gospel of Jesus Christ, and they (or their associates) baptize the new converts. The majority of these people are Gentiles, whose lifestyle is one of extreme immorality and decadence. They worship false gods. They have never heard of Abraham, Moses, or Jesus. They are heathens— sinful to the core.

The apostles then spend an average of six months with these new converts. They give them the fellowship of the body of Christ. They show them how to have a living, ongoing experience with an indwelling Lord. They teach them how to worship, how to meet, and how to care for one another's needs. They show them how to live by the life of Christ. They instruct them on how to have daily fellowship with the Lord and how to bring that fellowship into their homes, sharing it with one another in open-participatory meetings without stale ritual and without human headship.

The new church is born in glory. It's birthed in an explosion of freedom and joy. In only six months' time, the apostles convince these ex-pagans that they are holy in Christ. Their preaching produces an avalanche of heavenly glory.

After six months of drowning these new converts with an intoxicating unveiling of the Lord Jesus and their place in Him, the apostles leave the new church on its own. They leave it without any oversight, supervision, leadership, or administration.[14] They not only leave the church in its infancy, but they also leave it in a dangerously vulnerable position. You see, the church is living in a town that has utterly rejected these new Christians. They are social outcasts. They have been ostracized from their own culture and from their own people. And yet, the apostles leave them to the Holy Spirit and to the headship of the resurrected Christ.

Now ponder that scenario for a few moments.

And ask yourself: *Can I do that?*

Can you turn a group of heathen, immoral pagans into full-pledged Christians in six months? Can you present Jesus Christ in such profound depths that you can leave God's people awash with a sighting of His glorious face? Can you give the church a birth in heavenly glory, joy, and freedom? Do you possess that kind of high-octane, explosive, life-changing gospel? Can you show a group of new Christians how to have ongoing, daily fellowship with Christ and minister Him in its gatherings without a human being leading

---

14 Not all the churches that Paul planted had elders. But in those churches that did have elders, the elders always emerged much later. And they grew up organically. They were never present in the beginning.

or facilitating? Can you show them how to live by an indwelling Lord, out of which everything else flows? Can you teach them how to worship in homes without static ritual? Can you keep the church of the living God moving forward without resorting to legalism and without installing an organizational structure to control it? And when problems arise, can you handle them with the compassion, wisdom, and patience of Jesus Christ?

Can you do these things? If not, I will simply say to you that this is what has to be done if the Lord will see His dream fulfilled.

It is my conviction that all of the above is necessary if we are going to see a restoration of organic church life, which matches the heart of God. This brings us squarely to the issue of preparation. What does the New Testament teach about the preparation of an apostolic worker?

CHAPTER 3

THE MASTER PLAN OF CHURCH PLANTING

*The person who says it cannot be done should not
interrupt the person doing it.*

—Chinese proverb

How were church planters prepared for their ministry in the first
century?[1] Watchman Nee aptly writes,

> *Unless the man is right, right methods will be of no
> use to him or to his work.... In God's work everything
> depends upon the kind of worker sent out and the kind
> of convert produced.*[2]

---

1   I owe many of the insights in this chapter to Robert Coleman's *The Master Plan of Evangelism;* A. B.
Bruce's *The Training of the Twelve;* Stanley Grenz's *Theology for the Community of God;* Watchman Nee's
The Normal Christian Church Life; Gene Edwards' *Overlooked Christianity;* and David Shenk and Ervin
Stutzman's *Creating Communities of the Kingdom.*

2   Watchman Nee, *The Normal Christian Church Life* (Anaheim, CA: Living Stream Ministry, 1980),
xvii.

These words are as profound as they are true. And they go straight to the heart of God's method of raising up Christian workers. To paraphrase Nee, men look for methods, but God looks for men.[3]

Many contemporary Christians become highly enthused when they hear of a fancy new "method" or "scheme" to apply to God's work. But God is far more concerned with *the person* than He is with *the method*.

The Lord has a unique way of preparing His servants for His work. It's one that involves transformation. And transformation always involves emptying, suffering, and loss. Humanity's way is to hand you a method. Divinity's way is to hand you a cross.

A Root in Eternity

To understand how God prepares itinerant workers, we must begin at the starting point of the Christian life: eternity past. The pattern of the Christian life, the pattern of the church, and the pattern of church planting all have their roots in the triune God before time.

Before creation, there existed only God—a transcendent community of three Persons: Father, Son, and Spirit. Based on what we know from the New Testament, there were three things occurring within the Godhead in the dateless past.

- An exchange of divine life.

- An exchange of divine fellowship.

- A divine purpose to enlarge the life and fellowship to a creation called "humanity."

---

3   "Men" here includes women also. I'm using it to refer to "mankind" or "humankind."

Let me unfold that a bit.

First, the three Persons of the Godhead enjoyed an eternal exchange of divine life. The essence of that life is love. So within the Trinitarian Community, the Father, the Son, and the Spirit engaged in a divine dance of passionate and unconditional love for one another.

God is a community of perfect, mutual love. And this love is the very fountainhead of the divine nature (1 John 4:8, 16). For this reason, love is the essence of the Christian life. So we can say that the Christian life finds its roots in the Godhead in the dateless past (John 13:34–35; 17:23–25; Gal. 5:14; Rom. 13:8–10; 1 Tim. 1:5).

Second, the divine community enjoyed an eternal fellowship (Prov. 8:22–31; John 1:1–3, 18; 15:26; 17:5). The Father, Son, and Spirit mutually experienced what the New Testament calls *koinonia* (the shared life of the Spirit). *Koinonia* is the essence of organic church life. Biblically speaking, the church is a shared-life community whose members mutually fellowship with God and with one another (Acts 2:42; 1 Cor. 1:9; 2 Cor. 13:14; 1 John 1:3).

Consequently, the most primitive expression of the *ekklesia* is found in the fellowship of the Father, the Son, and the Spirit before time. We can say, then, that the church finds its origins in the Godhead in the timeless past. Theologian Stanley Grenz puts it this way,

> *As the doctrine of the Trinity asserts, throughout all eternity God is community, namely the fellowship of Father, Son, and Holy Spirit who comprise the triune God. The creation of humankind in the Divine*

image, therefore, can mean nothing less than that humans express the relational dynamic of God whose representation we are called to be.... The focus of this present experience, according to the New Testament writers, is the community of Christ.[4]

Understanding that the church flows out of the Godhead removes it from the world of human methodology. Church renewal, then, is not a matter of finding a new style, a new method, or a new structure. It's a matter of participating in God's life (2 Peter 1:4).

Third, the members of the Godhead counseled together and conceived an eternal purpose. They shrouded this purpose in a mystery, and they hid it in the Son until an appointed time (Rom. 16:25; Eph. 1:9–11; 3:3–11). What was that purpose? It was that the Trinitarian Community would one day expand its fellowship to others (John 17:20–26; Gal. 6:15; Eph. 2:15; 3:3–6; Col. 1:25–27; 3:11).

Herein lies the essence of apostolic work. It is to enlarge the circle of divine life and fellowship to human beings. When men and women are brought to Christ and organic churches are born, the divine fellowship is expanded. Properly understood, the church is a human community that lives by divine life and participates in and reflects the divine fellowship (John 6:57; Gal. 2:20; 2 Peter 1:4). As Stuart Murray says,

This story is the story of community. The Trinity, God in community, reaches out in creation and in

4   Stanley Grenz, *Theology for the Community of God* (Grand Rapids, MI: Eerdmans, 1994), 179.

redemption to form a human community to participate
in the Divine community.... Church planting is about
establishing new communities of faith.[5]

Stanley Grenz expands this point by saying,

Throughout eternity God is Father, Son, and Holy
Spirit—the community of love. More specifically, the
dynamic of the Trinity is the love shared between the
Father and the Son, which is the Holy Spirit. God's
purpose is to bring glory to His own triune nature by
establishing a reconciled creation in which humans
reflect the reality of the Creator. The triune God
desires that human beings be brought together into
a fellowship of reconciliation, which not only reflects
God's own eternal essence, but actually participates in
His nature (2 Peter 1:4).

So it's within the eternal Godhead that we find the headwaters
of the Christian life (divine life), the headwaters of organic church
life (divine fellowship), and the headwaters of apostolic work (the
divine plan of enlarging the life and fellowship that exists within the
Godhead). R. Paul Stevens puts it beautifully when he writes,

There was ministry before there was a world, ministry
in the being of God.... Ministry is God's ministry,
arising from the communal life of God, the Father,

---

5   Stuart Murray, *Church Planting: Laying Foundations* (Scottdale, PA: Herald, 2001), 170.

*Son and Spirit ministering love to one another even
before there was a world to save.*[6]

A Conception in Nazareth

It is in Jesus of Nazareth that we have the first glance of the Christian
life lived on planet earth. At an appointed time the Son of God
stepped out of the heavenly portals of glory and became a man. Born
in Bethlehem and raised in Nazareth, Jesus embodied God's eternal
thought for humanity. (This is the meaning of the Lord's oft-used
title "Son of Man.")

With the advent of the Lord Jesus on earth, what had its root
in eternity past was conceived in a carpenter's shop in the ill-reputed
town of Nazareth (John 1:46). It was in that carpenter's shop that
God the Father taught Jesus three things (Luke 2:40, 49, 52; 4:16):

- To live by divine life (the Christian life).

- To experience the fellowship of the divine
  community (organic church life).

- To enlarge the divine life and fellowship to
  others (apostolic work).

Let's unpack each point.

First, the Father taught His Son how to live by divine love (John
5:19–20, 26, 30; 7:16; 8:26, 28; 10:37–38; 12:49–50; 14:10). This

---

6   R. Paul Stevens, *The Abolition of the Laity* (Carlisle, PA: Paternoster, 1999), 141, 143.

is essentially the Christian life. The Christian life is a life lived by God's own life.

The Son showed forth God's idea for humanity. In God's thought, humans are God-created beings who are called to live by His life and express His love. The Son, therefore, brought to earth the unconditional love that He knew before His incarnation.

In this way, Jesus Christ expressed the image of God as a human. He revealed to men and angels how humans are to live: by the life of God. Very simply, Jesus Christ lived by means of His Father's indwelling life (John 6:57).[7]

Second, the Father taught the Son how to fellowship with Him as a man. In the days of His flesh, the Lord Jesus learned to fellowship with His Father internally.

As a man, Jesus Christ continued the divine *koinonia* that He once knew in eternity past. In Jesus, humanity had fellowship with divinity. For the first time a human being was brought into vital participation with the divine community. In this way, Jesus Christ incarnated God's purpose for humanity.

Third, the Father trained the Son how to be the first apostolic worker (John 4:34; 9:4; Heb. 3:1). Jesus learned from His Father how to build His church, the very organism that He would later give His life for (Matt. 16:18; Eph. 5:25).

Amazingly, Jesus did not learn how to build the church at the hands of religious specialists. The would-be scribes of His day formally studied the Hebrew Scriptures, the oral traditions, and the rabbinical commentaries under tutors. The would-be priests went

---

7   Incidentally, the way most modern believers are taught to live the Christian life is a poor fit to the way Christ demonstrated how to live it. Jesus did not try to be good; He lived by the indwelling life of His Father.

off to master the rituals of their sacred trade in Jerusalem. But Jesus learned how to be the first Christian worker as a blue-collar laborer in a lowly carpenter shop.

Jesus knew no seminary, no human tutors, and no academic program. Instead, He learned to fellowship with His Father, love His Father, obey His Father, and receive His Father's teaching amid the splinters and sawdust that lay amid a "layman's" workplace.

Therefore, what had its root within the Godhead in eternity past was conceived in the life of the Nazarene carpenter. The Christian life, the church, and apostolic work were all experienced within the God-man, Jesus of Nazareth. What God the Son knew in His eternal state was brought to earth without being altered, edited, or changed. The heavenly music that He sang in eternity was transposed from the divine key to the human key. But the song remained the same.

An Embryo in Galilee

As arresting as it may sound, it took the Father approximately thirty years to prepare His Son to be the first apostolic worker. The Lord Jesus did not begin His earthly ministry until He was empowered by the Spirit at about age thirty (Luke 3:22–23). This occurred at His baptism in the Jordan River (Matt. 3:16–17). Jesus Christ did no preaching, teaching, or healing before that time (Luke 4:1, 16–18).

Thus the Father *called* Jesus Christ, *prepared* Him for thirty years, and finally *sent* Him to accomplish His work.[8] As we will shortly see, being *called, prepared,* and *sent* is an unbroken spiritual principle that consistently runs throughout the New Testament narrative.

---

8   Granted, following His earthly ministry, our Lord accomplished His greatest work at Calvary. But because the scope of this chapter is our Lord's earthly life and ministry, we will not deal with His atoning work—which is unique to Him alone.

Let me insert a few words about calling and sending. A call to God's work is a call to divine service. It's not a call to meet a human need. And that call should be followed by a sending.

All genuine Christian workers should be sent. This implies that they do not take the initiative in God's work. Nor do they take it into their own hands. Those who take up God's work who aren't sent are volunteers. And God knows no volunteers when it comes to His work. There's a huge difference between a person who is *sent* and a person who *went*. I believe the Lord is raising up a new breed of Christian workers who will wait on their calling and their sending.

A worker's calling should be confirmed by representative members of the body of Christ who send him or her out. This principle keeps workers from being freelancing lone rangers in the kingdom of God.

Again, the word *apostle* in Greek literally means "one who is sent." All throughout the book of John, Jesus says that He is sent (4:34; 5:23–24, 30, 36–38; 6:29, 44, 57). The book of Hebrews calls Jesus an apostle (3:1). In fact, Jesus was the first apostle.

The sending of the Son holds tremendous significance for all who are called to God's work today. If Jesus, the first Christian worker, was sent, how much more should all workers after Him be sent? Watchman Nee eloquently observes,

> *The tragedy in Christian work today is that so many workers have simply gone out, they have not been sent. It is Divine commission that constitutes the call to Divine work. Personal desire, friendly persuasions, the advice of one's elders and the urge of opportunity—all*

> *these are factors on the natural plane, and they can*
> *never take the place of a spiritual call.... A Divine call*
> *gives God His rightful place, for it recognizes Him as*
> *the Originator of the work.*[9]

Let's now look at the Twelve. Shortly after Jesus began His earthly ministry, He *called* twelve men to work with Him (Matt. 4:19–21; 9:9; Mark 1:19–21; Luke 6:13). He *prepared* them for it. And He finally *sent* them to carry it out (Mark 3:13–14). So as the Father called, prepared, and sent the Son—so the Son called, prepared, and sent the Twelve (John 17:18).[10]

How did the Lord Jesus prepare the Twelve after He called them? The short answer is that He prepared them the same way that His Father prepared Him. There were essentially three leading elements in the Son's training of the Twelve. And they run parallel with what happened both in Nazareth and in eternity past. Jesus Christ taught the Twelve:

- How to live by divine life (the Christian life).

- How to experience the fellowship of the divine community (organic church life).

- How to expand the divine life and fellowship to others (apostolic work).

---

9   Watchman Nee, *The Normal Christian Church Life* (Anaheim, CA: Living Stream Ministry, 1980), 21–22.

10   There was also a band of women who followed the Lord along with the Twelve (Luke 8:2–3). It must be remembered, then, that women were part of the Galilean experience also.

Let's take a look at each of the above.

First, Jesus taught the Twelve how to live the Christian life. The essential ingredients in this teaching lay in the words "He appointed twelve—designating them apostles—that they might be with him" (Mark 3:14).

The Twelve lived with the Son of God. Day in and day out, they watched Him draw His life from His indwelling Father. They beheld the incomparable manner in which He denied Himself and poured out His life for others. They marveled at His peerless words, awed at His matchless compassion, wondered at His sagacious handling of criticism, studied His gracious responses to persecution, and scrutinized His heartfelt praying. As A. B. Bruce says,

> *In the training of the twelve for the work of apostleship, hearing and seeing the words and works of Christ necessarily occupied an important place. Eye and ear witnessing of the facts of an unparalleled life was an indispensable preparation for future witness-bearing.*[11]

In short, the Twelve watched a Man live by divine life. And this "watching" didn't take place from the sidelines. It happened in the heart of the playing field as the Twelve *lived* in the presence of the Son of God.

In this way, Jesus' mode of pedagogy represents a dramatic break with today's data-transfer model of teaching, where information is sterilely passed from one notebook to another. The Lord's way of

---

11   A. B. Bruce, *The Training of the Twelve* (Grand Rapids, MI: Kregel, 2000), 41.

training produces transformed disciples, while the modern method breeds isolated consumers of mental information.

Second, Jesus introduced the Twelve to the life of the church. That is, they learned to fellowship with Jesus and with one another in informal settings. They sat at His feet and listened to His words in homes, on seashores, along dusty roads, on mountaintops, and around campfires—asking Him questions and responding to His inquiries (Mark 4:10, 34; 7:17; Luke 8:9; 9:18; 11:1; John 6:3; 9:2). The Twelve consistently enjoyed table fellowship with one another while breaking bread with the Son of God in their midst (Matt. 26:26; Luke 24:41–43).

Interestingly, these activities are the chief features of the first church that was born a few years afterward (Acts 2:42). Hence, the primitive simplicity that the Twelve enjoyed with Jesus in Galilee was the embryo of the *ekklesia*. It was a foreshadowing of what was to come: humanity participating in the fellowship of divinity with Jesus Christ as Head. In a word, what happened in Galilee with Jesus and the Twelve was the embryonic experience of organic church life.

Third, the Lord trained the Twelve to be apostles—those who would found Christian communities. What did that training consist of? It certainly was not what natural minds would suspect. Contrary to the modern-day practice of preparing men and women for "the ministry," the Twelve did very little spiritual service while Jesus was on earth.

Granted, they had two trial missions that presumably lasted only a few weeks (Mark 6:7ff.; Luke 10:1ff.). They returned afterward and reported their experiences and received the Lord's feedback (Mark 6:30; Luke 9:10; 10:17ff.). However, the bulk of the Twelve's activities consisted of mundane tasks like distributing food to hungry multitudes, managing housing arrangements for the Lord's itinerant ministry, baptizing new converts, and preparing food for their journeys.

Jesus taught the Twelve how to fulfill God's work by modeling it before them daily. By His example, the Lord showed them the practical matters of prayer, service, self-denial, healing, showing compassion, handling conflict, and addressing questions. But the most important part of their training rested in their experience of corporate life under the Lord's direct headship.

Note that the Twelve not only lived with Jesus, but they also lived with one another. And through their experience of communal living, the Twelve were exposed. The carnality lurking in the shadows of their hearts surfaced as their wills collided. The dark sides of their personalities were laid bare as the Twelve chafed against one another (Matt. 8:25–26; 17:19–20; Mark 6:52; 10:13–14, 35–37, 41; 14:29–30; 16:14; Luke 9:46, 54; 22:24).

Jesus cut through their preconceived notions. Like a fine surgeon, He ripped into their souls and disclosed their ulterior motives. He dealt with their eccentricities. He rearranged their thinking about God, about the kingdom, about power, and about one another. He also taught them a great deal about each subject.

It was in that three-year period of living in an intense, shared-life community with Jesus Christ as Center that the Twelve were exposed, tried, and broken. It was within that corporate context that they learned the priceless lessons of relatedness, forbearance, patience, long-suffering, humility, forgiveness, dependence, and compassion. (Such lessons exact an obscenely high price.)

The Galilean experience was on-the-job training for the Twelve. The magnificent texture of that experience eventually qualified a dozen deeply fallen men to be useful in the Master's hands (Judas Iscariot being the exception). In short, the Galilean embryo of the church became the divine training ground for the Twelve. For this reason, the Galilean experience should never be underestimated. It establishes a pattern that will not move. Again, Robert Coleman writes,

> *Amazing as it may seem, all Jesus did to teach these men his way was to draw them close to himself. He was his own school and curriculum.... The time which Jesus invested in these few disciples was so much more by comparison to that given to others that it can only be regarded as a deliberate strategy. He actually spent more time with his disciples than with everybody else in the world put together. He ate with them, slept with them, and talked with them for the most part of his entire active ministry.... One must not overlook that even while Jesus was ministering to others, the disciples were always there with him.... Without any fanfare and unnoticed by the world, Jesus was saying that he had been training men to be his witnesses after he had gone, and his method of doing it was simply by being "with them."*[12]

I personally don't think we can improve upon Galilee in the training of young workers. Every man and woman who is called of the Lord to His work needs a Galilee in his or her experience. What Jesus Christ did with the Twelve is a reflection of God's way of raising up Christian workers.

A Birth in Jerusalem

After three years of living with and beholding the Son of God, the Twelve were sent by Jesus to begin their ministry of planting churches (Matt. 28:18–20; John 20:21). The twelve *disciples* became the twelve *apostles*—"sent ones."

After His resurrection, Christ breathed into the Twelve the very life that indwelt His own being. And twelve uneducated Galileans received an indwelling Lord (John 20:22). Once the Lord Jesus had fully prepared the Twelve, He left them on their own (John 14:28). In reality, however, He didn't leave them alone. He instead abandoned them to the Holy Spirit (John 16:7).

Hence, the Christ who they had once fellowshipped with in person had now come to dwell in them by the Spirit (John 14:16–18; 16:13–16). And just as Jesus Christ lived by an indwelling Father, the Twelve began to live by an indwelling Son. The passage had moved from the Father to the Son—then from the Son to the Twelve (John 17:18; 20:21).

On the day of Pentecost the church was birthed in Jerusalem, and three thousand souls were quickly added to it. The stewardship of God had now passed into the hands of the Twelve. The twelve apostles raised up the Jerusalem church by declaring Jesus Christ to unregenerate Jews and showing them how to live by His indwelling life.

Galilee had expanded into Jerusalem. And the Twelve passed on to the new converts in Jerusalem the same fellowship they had known with the Son of God—which was the same fellowship that the Son had known with His Father on earth as well as before creation (Acts 4:20; 1 John 1:1–3). For the first time, the church—the expanded community of divine life and fellowship—was born on earth. Theologian Clark Pinnock writes,

> *The church is meant to resemble the triune life by being itself a place of reciprocity and self-giving. The fellowship that we have with one another is related ultimately to our fellowship with Father and Son (1 John 1:3).... Fellowship refers to Divine life and to community life, because the community is meant to reflect the community of the Trinity, which is the ontological basis of the church.*[13]

R. Paul Stevens puts it this way:

> *God who is community of Father, Son, and Spirit has created a community that expresses God's love life on earth.*[14]

Over the next four years, the Lord began to secure a number of men in the Jerusalem church for His work. These men were exposed, broken, tried, and unwittingly trained in the corporate context of body life. And they began to surface as fit vessels in the Master's hands.

---

13   Clark Pinnock, *Flame of Love: A Theology of the Holy Spirit* (Downers Grove, IL: InterVarsity, 1996), 117.
14   R. Paul Stevens, *The Abolition of the Laity* (Carlisle, PA: Paternoster, 1999), 62.

Among this company were James (the Lord's brother), Stephen, Philip, Agabus, Silas, Judas, and Barnabas. These men emerged on the stage of the first-century drama as people who would later engage in itinerant ministry. (Barnabas, Silas, and James would later become apostles themselves.)

Notwithstanding, all of these men did not engage in Christian work until they first received years of experience in the church at Jerusalem. Thus the trek that these seven men walked mapped perfectly with that of the Twelve in Galilee. To summarize, the Twelve taught the believers in Jerusalem the following:

- How to live by divine life (the Christian life).

- How to experience the fellowship of the divine community (organic church life).

- How to expand the divine life and fellowship to others (apostolic work—particularly in relation to Barnabas, Silas, and James; Philip was an evangelist and Agabus a prophet).

A Walk in the Aegean World

What began inside the Godhead in eternity past was conceived within one Man in Nazareth. It developed as an embryo within a group of twelve men in Galilee. And it was born in the midst of three thousand converts in Jerusalem.

Yet this same principle continues unbroken throughout the pages of the New Testament. More than a decade after his conversion, Paul of Tarsus was sent out by the Holy Spirit along with Barnabas to the work of planting churches. And as was the case with all the workers who preceded them, Paul and Barnabas had spent a considerable amount of time learning Christ in the context of organic church life. That experience preceded their "being sent" to itinerant work. (Before they were sent, Barnabas had spent about eleven years in the Jerusalem assembly. Paul had spent about five years in the Antioch assembly.)[15]

In addition, just as Barnabas was prepared by living with and observing the Twelve in Jerusalem, Paul was prepared by living with and observing Barnabas in Antioch.[16] Both Paul and Barnabas were clearly *called* by God to His work. In his letters, Paul repeatedly testifies that he was called to be an apostle (Gal. 1:1; Eph 1:1; Col. 1:1; 1 Tim. 1:1; 2:7; 2 Tim. 1:11). The New Testament is quite clear that Barnabas was also an apostle (Acts 14:3–4, 14; 1 Cor. 9:5–6).

Paul and Barnabas stood in a long lineage of itinerant workers who were called, prepared, and then sent. Interestingly, just as the *Father* sent the Son ... and just as the *Son* sent the Twelve ... so the *Spirit* sent Paul and Barnabas (Acts 13:4). And it is the Spirit who still sends workers today.

In short, the Twelve taught Barnabas the following:

---

15   In Antioch, Paul quickly matured to be a prophet/teacher along with Barnabas (Acts 13:1). Apostles, therefore, are first brothers. They then grow to manifest their gifts as prophets or teachers or evangelists, etc. They are then sent out to use their gifts to plant churches. Not all prophets, teachers, and evangelists become apostles ("sent ones"). But apostles are often prophets, teachers, and/or evangelists before they are sent.

16   This seems clear from the fact that the more experienced Barnabas searched for Saul in Tarsus and brought him to Antioch to help with the work there (Acts 11:25ff.). Also, Luke makes clear by his wording that Barnabas took the lead ahead of Paul until the two men got to Paphos (Acts 13:13, 42–43, et al.). Before this point, Luke always mentions Barnabas's name ahead of Paul's. Afterward, he always says "Paul and Barnabas." See F. F. Bruce, *The Pauline Circle* (Grand Rapids, MI: Eerdmans, 1985), 18–19; Watchman Nee, *Church Affairs* (Richmond, VA: Christian Fellowship Publishers, 1982), 135–41.

- ✤ How to live by divine life (the Christian life).

- ✤ How to experience the fellowship of the divine community (organic church life).

- ✤ How to expand the divine life and fellowship to others (apostolic work).

And Barnabas taught Paul the following:

- ✤ How to live by divine life (the Christian life).

- ✤ How to experience the fellowship of the divine community (organic church life).

- ✤ How to expand the divine life and fellowship to others (apostolic work).

Later, Paul traveled with Silas to plant churches in Greece (Acts 15—18). Like Paul and Barnabas, Silas was called to the work, he was prepared in the Jerusalem church along with Barnabas, and he was sent. The New Testament makes clear that Silas (also called Silvanus) was also an apostle (1 Thess. 1:1; 2:6).

Galilee Is Duplicated in Ephesus

This principle of being called, prepared, and sent didn't end with Paul, Barnabas, or Silas. Paul raised up churches in Galatia, Macedonia, Achaia, and Asia Minor (Acts 13—20). He modeled the Christian life to his new converts (1 Cor. 4:16; 11:1; 2 Thess. 3:7–9). And he trained those who were called to be apostolic workers (Acts 20:1–4; 1 Cor. 4:17; 1 Tim. 1:2; 2 Tim. 2:1–2).

In his later years, Paul trained young workers in the city of Ephesus in the same way that Jesus trained the Twelve in Galilee. In effect, Paul duplicated the Galilean experience of Jesus and the twelve apostles in the city of Ephesus. David Shenk and Ervin Stutzman write,

> *Paul's strategy for leadership training is not unlike that of Jesus.... Every church planter should do the same.... This needs to be a foundational commitment of every church planter: plant churches and train others to do the same.*[17]

Note that each man whom Paul trained experienced organic church life first as a brother and not as a leader or a minister. To be more specific:

- Titus lived in organic church life in Antioch, Syria, for a period of years.

- Timothy lived in organic church life in Lystra for a period of years.

- Gaius lived in organic church life in Derbe for a period of years.

---

17 David Shenk and Ervin Stutzman, *Creating Communities of the Kingdom* (Scottdale, PA: Herald, 1988), 157–58.

- ❧ Aristarchus lived in organic church life in Thessalonica for a period of years.

- ❧ Secundus lived in organic church life in Thessalonica for a period of years.

- ❧ Sopator lived in organic church life in Berea for a period of years.

- ❧ Tychicus lived in organic church life in Ephesus for a period of years.

- ❧ Trophimus lived in organic church life in Ephesus for a period of years.

This was their spiritual preparation. These eight men watched an apostle raise up a church bare-handed in the great city of Ephesus.

If you recall, the Twelve whom Jesus trained learned by "being with" and "beholding" the Lord (Mark 3:14; John 1:14; 1 John 1:1–3). So, too, the eight men whom Paul trained learned in the same way (Acts 19:1—20:4). Again, David Shenk and Ervin Stutzman observe,

> *For several years, Timothy learned from Paul by watching him work and by assisting him in his work. He was with Paul in Philippi when they met with Lydia and the women at the river.... He witnessed Paul being beaten and imprisoned, and he saw God's miraculous intervention in the earthquake..... In all these experiences Timothy watched Paul and worked*

with him. He "saw" and "did" ministry in partnership
with Paul not only in Philippi, but in subsequent
church planting in other cities.[18]

As was true in Paul's own life, the men Paul trained were: (1) *called* by God, (2) *prepared* in the context of organic church life, and (3) *sent* by the Spirit through Paul himself (Acts 16:1–3; 19:22; 1 Cor. 4:17; 1 Thess. 3:1–2). To be more specific, Paul's eight apprentices learned the following from Paul and from the churches in which they lived. They learned:

- How to live by divine life (the Christian life).

- How to experience the fellowship of the divine community (organic church life).

- How to expand the divine life and fellowship to others (apostolic work).

Thus the divine principle of being called, prepared, and sent unshakably holds throughout the entire New Testament. It's a consistent line that's rooted in the Godhead before time. It was brought to earth by Jesus and moved from Jesus all the way to Paul and his coworkers. The pattern cannot be broken. And in my opinion, we are unwise to presume that we can improve upon it.

---

18   David Shenk and Ervin Stutzman, *Creating Communities of the Kingdom* (Scottdale, PA: Herald, 1988), 152.

CHAPTER 4

APOSTOLIC COVERING VS. APOSTOLIC HELP

Men occasionally stumble over the truth, but most pick themselves up and hurry on as if nothing had happened.

—Winston Churchill

In this chapter, we will explore the anatomy of apostolic authority. The commission of an apostolic worker is *personal*. But his sending out must be *corporate*. An apostolic worker is usually a teacher, prophet, or evangelist who has been directly called by God to a regional work. He has also been publicly sent out by a local group of believers.

It's this inward commission and outward sending that constitute one an apostle. Workers can also be sent out by the hand of an older worker who mentors them (1 Cor. 4:17; 2 Cor. 8:16–23; 12:18; Eph. 6:21–22; Col. 4:7–8; 1 Thess. 3:1–2; 2 Tim. 4:12; Titus 3:12–13).

Again, the Greek word *apostolos*, often translated "apostle," literally means one who is sent forth. Therefore, the New Testament knows nothing of a *self*-appointed, *self*-anointed, *self*-sent apostle.

Apostolic workers, in the New Testament sense, are itinerant, mobile, translocal people who critique the culture, proclaim the gospel, and plant and nurture *ekklesias*. Just how they accomplish these tasks and how much authority they wield are questions that we'll consider in this chapter.

The Question of Apostolic Covering

In *Reimagining Church*, I discuss in detail the notion of spiritual and "denominational covering." Similar to "denominational covering," but having a flair all of its own, is the notion of "apostolic covering."

According to this teaching, a church is protected from doctrinal error if it submits to a contemporary apostle. It rests upon the idea that apostolic workers have official authority to control and direct the affairs of a church.

The Bible, however, runs contrary to this idea. Nowhere in the New Testament do we find an apostle assuming the full responsibility of a local church once the foundation has been fully laid. Rather, the apostles of the New Testament both recognized and respected the spiritual autonomy of each church once it was established.

Granted, the church was in the hands of the apostle while he was laying the foundation. But the responsibility fell into the hands of the whole church once he departed. *And he always departed.*

In the beginning of a church's life, the burden of oversight belongs to the apostolic worker or apostolic team. It then shifts to the elders once they emerge. Apostolic workers are responsible for their own regional ministries. But the church is responsible for its own local affairs.

Again, when an apostolic worker is giving birth to a church, the church is in his hands. Such a period can be likened to an incubation phase. The worker spends time ministering Christ to the believers and equipping them for ministry. While under house arrest, Paul was able to rent his own home to conduct apostolic meetings in Rome alongside the meetings of the church (Acts 28:30–31).

Paul did something similar when he was in Ephesus. He held apostolic meetings in the Hall of Tyrannus, while the local believers gathered in homes (Acts 19:9; 20:20; 1 Cor. 16:19). Such apostolic meetings were meetings of *the work*. And they were designed to equip the saints to function as *the church*. Yet once the worker laid the foundation and left the church on its own, he transferred all oversight and responsibility into the hands of the local believers.

While Paul sometimes spent an extended length of time to plant a church (Corinth—eighteen months; Ephesus—three years), he always left the churches on their own once the foundation was established. And after leaving, he didn't meddle in the church's affairs—though he was always available to help and encourage.

In like manner, Antioch served as Paul's home base for his first two apostolic journeys. Yet he didn't dominate the church's affairs while there. In Antioch, Paul was simply a respected brother with a recognized gift of teaching and preaching. He was not an apostle to that church.

This explains why the New Testament mentions the elders of Ephesus, the elders of Jerusalem, the overseers of Philippi, etc. But it never mentions the apostles of these places. While the Twelve resided in Jerusalem as a home base for their ministry during the initial season of the church's existence, the New Testament never calls them "the apostles *of* Jerusalem."

Again, the apostolic ministry, or "the work," exists as a separate entity from the churches. The work is regional. The churches are local. The work is transient. The churches are settled. The work is a roving association. The churches are resident communities. Apostolic workers are travelers, not settlers. They are pioneers, not stationaries.

Typically, Paul would spend several months establishing the ground floor of a believing community, only to leave it to itself for lengthy periods of time. While away from the church, he was available to offer advice (1 Cor. 7:1). He also made periodic visits to check on its progress and to strengthen its life (Acts 15:36; 18:23; 2 Cor. 12:14; 13:1). However, he never took charge of its affairs. (More on that later.)

The practice of leaving churches in their infancy reveals the daunting fact that Paul believed the church to be a living organism that would develop on its own by the power of God's life. He knew how to plant a church in such a way that when he left it, the Spirit would remain active within the community.

At the same time, the churches that Paul planted received help from other churches (Acts 16:2; 1 Thess. 1:7–8). They also stayed in steady contact with Paul. In fact, even after twelve years, the church in Philippi still needed the spiritual assistance of their founding apostle (Phil. 1:23–27).

There is massive confusion today among Christians between "the work" and "the church." As we have already seen, the two are distinct and must be kept along their own respective lines. For example, when church leaders teach that every Christian is a "missionary" and that the goal of a local church is to break up and create many new churches, which in turn, should create many other new churches, then the church is being co-opted by the work. The truth is, not all Christians are sent out to the apostolic work (see chapter 1) and not all are called to be apostles (1 Cor. 12:28ff.; Eph. 4:11ff.).

Also, when a Christian worker sets up his home base in a local church and dominates its life and ministry, then the work has taken over the church. The church becomes nothing more than an extension of the worker's own ministry. As long as he is resident and very involved, there will be an unhealthy mingling of the church and the work. The church, in effect, becomes the franchise of the worker.

The work exists for the churches—not for its own sake. In fact, the work produces the churches. At the same time, the churches produce workers in time. The work is never to rival, substitute, or overshadow the church. The goal of the work is to establish and strengthen the churches. So the church—which is the corporate expression of Jesus Christ in a given locale—is both the goal and the means of God's grand mission.[1] God desires to fill the earth with His Son (Eph. 1:10, 23; 4:10). The way He does this is by giving birth to organic Christian communities by means of the apostolic work.

In a word, apostolic workers are responsible for planting and nurturing churches in many different places. Genuine apostolic workers never permanently settle down in the churches they plant. Nor do they assume exclusive authority over them.

---

1   This statement is fully developed in my book *From Eternity to Here*.

Church Planters or Church Supplanters?

Although the early apostles were valued servants to the early churches, they were not usurpers (1 Cor. 4:1). They didn't conduct themselves as resident chairmen or distant bosses over God's people.

Put another way, first-century apostles were church *planters*—not *supplanters*. They were assistants, not spiritual aristocrats. Servants, not ecclesiastical despots. Foundation layers, not high-powered celebrity figures. While first-century apostles instructed and persuaded the churches, they never controlled them.

While some today have glamorized the apostolic vocation, Paul considered apostles to be the "last of all … fools … weak … without honor … the scum of the world, the dregs of all things" (1 Cor. 4:9–13 NASB). True workers, therefore, are not glory-grabbers. They do not seek to impress people (2 Cor. 11:5–6; 1 Thess. 2:5–6). They do not seek financial gain (2 Cor. 2:17; 11:9). Nor do they dominate the lives of others (2 Cor. 1:24).

True workers don't claim impressive credentials (2 Cor. 3:1–3). They do not assert a superior heritage (2 Cor. 11:21–22). Nor do they boast of extraordinary spiritual experiences (2 Cor. 10:12–15; 11:16–19; 12:1, 12).

For Paul, apostolic workers are not self-appointed, self-advancing, spiritual elitists. Rather, they are those who shovel the dung after the procession ends. They spill their blood for God's house.

The grabbing of power and the exertion of oneself over others is not apostleship ("sent-ness"). It's just another stale, warmed-over version of oppression. Real workers are first and foremost servants.

Consequently, instead of deploying imperial metaphors, Paul draws metaphors from the family to describe his relationship to the churches he worked with. To the churches, Paul is a father, a mother, and a nurse (1 Cor. 3:2; 4:14–15; 2 Cor. 12:14; Gal. 4:19; 1 Thess. 2:7, 11), not a lord, a master, or a king.

Likewise, the persuasive overtones that permeate Paul's letters show that he treated the churches as a father would treat his *adult* children as opposed to his toddlers. As a spiritual father, he gave his judgment on church affairs. But he didn't issue unilateral decrees.

In effect, the churches that Paul planted progressively moved away from dependence upon him. They rather grew in their dependence upon Christ (1 Cor. 2:1–5). And Paul urged them in this path (1 Cor. 14:20; Eph. 4:14).

The Pauline Pattern

One of the most dynamic features of Paul's pattern of church planting was his consistent subjection to other Christians. From the outset of his conversion, Paul learned to depend upon his fellow brethren. His first lesson of subjection to the body was with Ananias. Ananias was the brother at whose hands Paul received the Spirit and a confirmation of his calling (Acts 9:17–19; 22:12–16).

Subsequently, Paul was sent away by the believers in Berea (Acts 17:14). He was strengthened by his colaborers in Corinth (Acts 18:5). He was restrained by the saints at Ephesus (Acts 19:30). He was also advised by the brothers in Jerusalem (Acts 21:23). In a word, Paul knew how to receive help and enrichment from other Christians (Rom. 15:32; 1 Cor. 16:18; Phil. 2:19; 2 Tim. 1:16).

While he was certainly endowed with a seasoned spiritual history and many powerful gifts, Paul regarded his authority as functional and relational—not official or sacral. For Paul, spiritual authority was rooted in the Lord's approval, not in some formal office (2 Cor. 10:18).

This explains why Paul virtually always sought to *persuade* the churches concerning God's mind rather than issuing imperial commands. In fact, Paul's two favorite words for addressing the saints are *parakalein* and *erotao*. *Parakalein* means an appeal. *Erotao* means a request made between equals.

In the same strain, Paul refrained from using the very strong word *epitage* (commandment) to charge obedience to himself (1 Cor. 7:6, 25; 2 Cor. 8:8; Philem. 8–9).

When Paul called the believers to action or attitude, we find him "urging," "beseeching," "pleading," "appealing," and "asking" rather than issuing authoritarian decrees. Paul's letters are dripping with this kind of cooperative tone (Rom. 12:1; 15:30; 16:2, 17; 1 Cor. 1:10; 4:16; 16:12, 15; 2 Cor. 2:8; 5:20; 6:1; 8:6; 9:5; 10:1–2; 12:18; Gal. 4:12; Eph. 3:13; 4:1; Phil. 4:2–3; 1 Thess. 2:3, 11; 4:1, 10; 5:12, 14; 2 Thess. 2:1; 3:14–15; 1 Tim. 1:3; 2:1; Philem. 9–10, 14).

To Paul's mind, the voluntary consent of his audience and their internalization of truth were far more desirable than nominal obedience to the things he wrote. At times when his tone was needfully sharp, Paul charged the believers to commend obedience to Christ rather than to himself (Rom. 1:5; 16:19, 26; 2 Cor. 2:9; Phil. 2:12).

On rare occasions he did charge (*paraggello*) obedience to the things that he had written (1 Thess. 4:11; 2 Thess. 3:4, 6, 10, 14). But the object of obedience was not Paul as a person. It was Christ whose mind he was expressing at the time.

Put another way, whenever Paul manifested the mind of Christ, his words were *authoritative*. But Paul himself was never *authoritarian*. Consider the following texts:

> *And unto the married I command, yet not I, but the Lord. (1 Cor. 7:10 KJV)*

> *If any man think himself to be a prophet, or spiritual, let him acknowledge that the things that I write unto you are the commandments of the Lord. (1 Cor. 14:37 KJV)*

> *For we are not as many, which corrupt the word of God: but as of sincerity, but as of God, in the sight of God speak we in Christ. (2 Cor. 2:17 KJV)*

> *For we preach not ourselves, but Christ Jesus the Lord; and ourselves your servants for Jesus' sake. (2 Cor. 4:5 KJV, see also 2 Cor. 11:19; 13:3–4; 1 Thess. 2:13; 4:2, 15; 2 Thess. 3:12)*

So Paul was not an authoritarian personality. Nor was he an independent freelancer. From his own lips, he made clear that he didn't regard his apostolic calling a license to dominate the affairs of the churches. And Paul never exploited his right as an apostle to receive financial help from those he served (1 Cor. 9:1–19).

In fact, his abiding principle was to refuse funds from those churches that he was serving at the time. Paul accepted money only from believers in other locales so as not to burden those who were recipients of his immediate help (2 Cor. 11:7–9).

In effect, Paul's whole outlook of apostolic authority is crystallized in the statement "Not that we have dominion over your faith, but are fellow workers for your joy " (2 Cor. 1:24 NKJV). Eugene Peterson paraphrases this passage as follows: "We're not in charge of how you live out the faith, looking over your shoulders, suspiciously critical. We're partners, working alongside you, joyfully expectant. I know that you stand by your own faith, not by ours" (MSG). In this way, Paul differed immeasurably from his opponents (2 Cor. 11:19–21).

The Source of Paul's Authority

The authority that Paul possessed was tied to his ability to speak the word of the Lord to the communities he founded. This is why it was an authority designed to build up rather than to tear down (2 Cor. 10:8; 13:10). Paul, therefore, always exercised authority for the sole purpose for which it was given—to edify the saints. He never misused it to gain prominence, earthly power, or material advantage.

Paul recognized that the source of his authority was Christ Himself as He is embodied in the gospel. This explains why he consistently invited the churches to judge what he said (1 Cor. 10:15; 11:13; 1 Thess. 5:21). Paul even urged them to reject his message if it was not consistent with the gospel (Gal. 1:8–9).

In like manner, the New Testament authors as a whole consistently exhort the churches to obey the raw truth of the gospel as it is found in Jesus Christ. The words of mere humans are not to be obeyed at face value (Rom. 6:17; Gal. 3:1; 5:7; Titus 1:14).

Paul expected the churches to give him a hearing insofar as his words reflected the gospel of Christ (Gal. 1:9) and insofar as they were in harmony with the Spirit of God (1 Cor. 7:40). Indeed, Paul was forced to reprove the churches on occasion. But he always found this difficult to do.

His reticence for giving rebuke is disclosed in his Corinthian correspondence. There we discover that Paul preferred to approach God's people with a spirit of gentleness rather than with a word of reproof (1 Cor. 4:21b). Yet when he had to address them sternly, he did so with much anguish of heart (2 Cor. 2:4).[2] Paul's love for the Corinthians was so overflowing with fatherly compassion that after he wrote them, he feared that his words may have been too strong (2 Cor. 7:8). Clearly, the consuming motivation that drove Paul to labor tirelessly and suffer for the churches was his surpassing love for God's people (2 Cor. 12:15; Phil. 2:17–21; Col. 1:24; 1 Thess. 2:8).

Because Paul often spoke the word of the Lord, he could say that those who rejected his words did not reject him but Christ (1 Thess. 4:8)—for to Paul's mind, "God has given us His Holy Spirit" (4:8b NKJV). Yet even in those times when the word of the Lord was in his mouth, Paul wanted the believers to acknowledge that what he said was the Lord's thoughts rather than his own (1 Cor. 14:37–38). The fact that Paul appealed to his faithful service as a basis for the saints' trust is unmistakable (1 Cor. 4:1–5; 7:25; 15:10; 2 Cor. 1:12; 4:1–2). Such service was an example to the churches (1 Cor. 4:16; Gal. 4:12; Phil. 3:17; 4:9; 2 Thess. 3:7).

---

2   Incidentally, Paul's "rod" in 1 Cor. 4:21 (KJV) is a metaphor for a word of rebuke rather than a token of forced subordination or unilateral authority (2 Cor. 10:3–6).

All of these facts embody the following sound insight: The *source* of spiritual authority is Christ. The *means* of spiritual authority is the Word of God. The *exercise* of spiritual authority is brokenness and servanthood. And the *goal* of spiritual authority is edification.

In God's thought, authority and the spirit of the cross go hand in hand. This principle is exhibited throughout Paul's apostolic ministry.

It should be understood that the canonical (biblical) writings penned by Paul and the other apostles are inspired and authoritative in their own right. They embody God's voice in Holy Scripture. In this chapter, however, we have been looking at Paul's writings with an eye to understanding the relationship between a worker and a church. When we look at Paul's letters through this lens, we discover that he was nonauthoritarian.

Granted, God gave Paul the responsibility to care for the churches he planted in multiple ways. But he was noncontrolling and noncoercive in all of them. As Robert Banks says,

> *Paul exercises authority among his communities by persuading them to accept his point of view. He does not try to coerce his converts. His persuasion is based on his capacity to convince them, by word and example, that he desires for them only what the gospel requires....*
> *Through the Spirit, God continues to speak and work authoritatively, not through coercion of people's personalities but by convincing their minds of truth and warming their hearts with love so that they freely embrace it.*

To Whom Does the Church Belong?

In all that Paul did to care for and protect a church, he acted in the capacity of a spiritual father and mother. Consider his words:

> *But we were gentle among you, like a mother caring for her little children. We loved you so much that we were delighted to share with you not only the gospel of God but our lives as well, because you had become so dear to us.... For you know that we dealt with each of you as a father deals with his own children, encouraging, comforting and urging you to live lives worthy of God, who calls you into his kingdom and glory. (1 Thess. 2:7–12)*

> *And I will not be burdensome to you; for I do not seek yours, but you. (2 Cor. 12:14 NKJV)*

Yet even though Paul took fatherly/motherly responsibility to care for the churches he established, he didn't see them as his franchise. Judging from the New Testament epistles, whenever Paul wrote to a church, he never once stated or implied that he had formal possession of it. The churches "belong" to God, to Christ, and to the believers. A church only belonged to Paul in the sense that children belong to their parents. Consider the following:

Galatians

🌿 Paul says the church belongs to Christ twice.

- He says the church belongs to the family of believers once.

- He calls the church "brethren" eleven times.

- He describes himself as a mother who has travailed in birth for the church.

1 Thessalonians

- Paul calls the church "brethren" seventeen times.

- He says he treated the members as a father treats his children.

- He says that he was gentle among them as a mother is with her children.

2 Thessalonians

- Paul calls the church "brethren" seven times.

1 Corinthians

- Paul calls the church "brethren" twenty-eight times.

- He says the church belongs to God twice.

- He says the church belongs to Christ once.

- He calls the members his children.

- He says he belongs to them.

- He says he is a servant to them.

- He uses the imagery of a mother who fed them with milk.

- He says that he is their only father who gave them birth through the gospel.

2 Corinthians

- Paul calls the church "brethren" eight times.

- He calls the members his children.

- He says he stored up for them as parents do for their children.

- He says he is a father who will present the church to Christ as a chaste virgin.

- He says he is not a lord over them, but a helper of their joy.

Romans

- He calls the church "brethren" fourteen times.

- He says the members belong to Christ.

Colossians

- He calls the church "brethren" two times.

Ephesians

- He calls the church "brethren" two times.

Philippians

- He calls the church "brethren" eight times.

The Nonauthoritarianism of Other Apostles

Timothy was as nonauthoritarian as Paul. Paul never gave his young coworker license to exert formal power over the saints. He rather encouraged Timothy to "exhort" them in meekness. Paul also instructed Timothy to cultivate a family-like relationship with the church (1 Tim. 5:1–2; 2 Tim. 2:24–25; 4:2).

In one place, Paul instructs Timothy with the words "These things command [*paraggello*] and teach" (1 Tim. 4:11 KJV). But the things that Paul exhorts Timothy to "command" are the words of the Holy Spirit (4:1). And they are informed by sound teaching (4:6). Like Paul, Timothy worked *with*, not *over*, God's people.

Paul's admonition to Titus is similar. In Titus 2:15, Paul's charge to "teach, exhort, and reprove these things with all authority [*epitage*]" is to be understood against the backdrop of his earlier injunction. That injunction was: "But as for you, speak the things which are fitting for sound doctrine" (Titus 2:1 NASB). In other words, Titus was free to authoritatively speak, reprove, and exhort those things that mirror the sound teaching of Jesus Christ. (For authority is vested in the latter.)

The letters of John breathe the same nonauthoritarian air. Like Paul, John didn't meddle in church affairs. Nor did he claim a right to rule the saints. When Diotrephes was usurping authority in one church, John did not seek to force him out. He rather exhorted the saints not to follow those who do evil (3 John 9–11).

John concedes that he has no commandment to give (1 John 2:7; 2 John 5–6). Instead, he points to Christ's new commandment—which is love. In all these ways, John's outlook on authority is parallel with Paul's.

Again, the inescapable conclusion in all this is that apostolic workers do not have official authority over churches. They do not assume formal possession of them. Nor do they turn them into franchises (or virtual denominations) of their own peculiar ministries.

Apostolic workers, if authentic, use their ministries to serve the churches. They do not use the churches to build their ministries.

The ministry of the first-century apostle, then, was a service rather than an expression of dominance. This is why Paul referred to the churches he planted in explicitly nonhierarchical terms. He called them "brethren" and "partners" in ministry (2 Cor. 5:20—6:1; 7:3; Phil. 1:5, 7; 2:17). When he spoke to them, he spoke as one of their own—as an equal. He did not speak as one who was above or over them (1 Cor. 5:2–3; Col. 2:5).

In this way, New Testament apostles did not control the churches. Neither did the churches control the apostles. Paul's words in Galatians 4:12 capture the thrust of his cooperative and relational mind-set: "Become as I am, for I also have become as you are" (NASB).

Paul's Confidence in the Churches

Paul had great confidence in the churches he planted. He was confident that they would function properly in his absence. Consider the following texts:

> I have confidence in you in the Lord that you will adopt no other view. (Gal. 5:10 NASB)

*We have confidence in the Lord that you are doing
and will continue to do the things we command.
(2 Thess. 3:4)*

*I had confidence in all of you, that you would all share
my joy. (2 Cor. 2:3)*

*I am glad I can have complete confidence in you.
(2 Cor. 7:16; see also 2 Cor. 8:22; Rom. 15:14;
Philem. 21; Phil. 1:6; Heb. 6:9)*

Even in the midst of the chaotic meetings at Corinth, Paul
never once put a choke hold on the church's open-participatory
gatherings. Nor did he prohibit the brethren from exercising
their gifts. Rather, he gave them broad guidelines to facilitate
the orderliness of their meetings. And he trusted that they would
adhere to them (1 Cor. 14:1ff.).

Paul had complete confidence in his ministry. So much so that he
trusted the churches to have open-participatory meetings without any
human officiation—including his own. In this way, Paul built well. He
worked toward equipping the saints to function in his absence.

Paul's Relationship with His Coworkers

Let's shift our attention to Paul's relationship with his coworkers.
How did Paul treat those who were part of his apostolic team?

Spiritual authority was expressed within the sphere of apostolic
work. And Paul was the center of his apostolic band. (Note that Paul
and the other workers were not independent freelancers. They always

moved in association with a circle of colaborers. This is virtually never the case with today's self-advancing "apostles.")

Paul clearly took responsibility for the direction of the work. He also had no problem administering the movements of his coworkers (Acts 16:1–4, 9–10; 17:15; 19:21–22; 20:3–5, 13–15; 1 Cor. 4:17; 2 Cor. 8:18–23; Eph. 6:21–22; Phil. 2:19, 23, 25, 28; Col. 4:8–9; 2 Tim. 4:9–13, 20–22; Titus 1:5; 3:12–13). Yet a fixed hierarchical system did not work among Paul's company. Paul was not the president or CEO of the work.

For this reason we never see Paul demanding his colaborers to thoughtless obedience. As with the churches, Paul sought the voluntary consent of his colleagues whenever he made a request of them (1 Cor. 16:10–12; 2 Cor. 8:6, 16–18; 9:5; 12:18; Phil. 2:22–23).

At times, Paul subjected himself to the wishes of his fellow workers (1 Cor. 16:12). He also allowed room for them to disagree with him (Acts 15:36–41). The sending of Titus mentioned in 2 Corinthians 8:17 underscores the participatory relationship that Paul had with his coworkers: "For he [Titus] not only accepted our appeal, but being himself very earnest, he has gone to you of his own accord" (NASB).

Paul took the lead in the sphere of his apostolic work simply because he was more spiritually advanced than his coworkers. It was not because he had a higher position in the ecclesiastical pyramid. Cooperation rather than authoritarianism marked Paul's dealings with his colaborers.

Because Paul exerted spiritual authority in the work, subjection in Paul's circle was voluntary and personal. It was never formal or official. Strikingly, Paul didn't regard the original Twelve as having some sort of hierarchical authority over him. Nor did he have any regard for "apostolic" status (Gal. 2:6–9). Recall that on one occasion, Paul rebuked one of the most prominent apostles in public when an essential truth was at stake (Gal. 2:11–21).

Apostles Are Dependent on the Body

The notion that holds that apostolic workers have ruling authority over local churches is untenable. So is the idea that some workers have official authority over other workers. These ideas are inventions of natural minds, and they are dissonant with Paul's actual practice.

Apostolic workers, just like all other ministries in the body of Christ, are dependent upon the body to receive Christ's fullness. This is clear from Paul's opening words to the Romans. There he states that he is eager not only to bless them by his gifts (1:11), but also to receive help through theirs (1:12; 15:32).

We do well to remember that God always condemns independence and individualism. Dependence upon God never renders us independent of one another. The Lord doesn't permit His people to "do what is right in their own eyes" (Deut. 12:8). And "he who separates himself seeks his own way and quarrels against all sound wisdom" (Prov. 18:1).

God, therefore, has not consigned any of us, including workers, into a little cubicle of our own existence where we may choose our own way. Those who conceive of their relationship with the Lord as wholly vertical ("me and Jesus alone") are deceived and fulfill the words of the sage: "The way of a fool is right in his own eyes, but a wise man is he who listens to counsel" (Prov. 12:15 NASB).

No matter how spiritual a Christian may be, he or she is never exempted from his or her need for the spiritual supply of his or her brothers and sisters in Christ. For even the mighty Moses needed the help of Aaron and Hur to strengthen his hands in the evil day (Ex. 17:10–13).

Of course, all that has been said is not tantamount to denying that apostolic workers do possess spiritual authority. They do. But again, spiritual authority is something far different from positional/hierarchal authority.

In the Lord, authority exists. But it's attached to function, not office. There is a tremendous difference between responding to function and responding to office. Office separates brethren. But Spirit-bestowed function builds them together.

As we have seen, Paul's letters clearly display a nonauthoritarian mind at work. They are also saturated with a cooperative tone. Yet because many modern Christians come to the New Testament with the preconceived idea that apostles have tremendous delegated authority, they miss the nonauthoritarian strain that liberally flows from Paul's pen. For this reason, today's popular notion of apostolic authority is unquestionably non-Pauline.

Apostolic Ministry Today

There is no shortage of self-styled, self-appointed, self-anointed, post-Pauline "apostles" running to and fro in the body of Christ today. Such people issue authoritarian decrees, claim followers, and build empires. As a result, many discerning Christians have concluded that apostles do not exist anymore.

Let it be known, however, that God has raised up genuine apostolic workers in this century. These are those who have walked—and are walking—in a Pauline spirit. Like Paul, these workers are not interested in building Christian empires nor in starting movements. Neither do they have any interest in reaching celebrity status or protecting their legacies (1 Cor. 1:13; 3:7, 21).

What, then, does a contemporary apostolic worker look like? If you are part of the institutional church scene, you may have never seen one. Yes, you have undoubtedly seen those who claim to be apostles. At the very least, you have heard of men who had the word *apostle* wrapped around them by others. Yet such men frequently lack the goods of a genuine worker.

By contrast, authentic workers are those who *hide* themselves rather than *hustle* themselves. Their work is largely unseen; their service frequently unnoticed. Real workers do not build denominations, programs, missions, buildings, or parachurch organizations. They exclusively build the *ekklesia* of Jesus Christ. And God uses the humble in heart to build His house (Isa. 66:1–2).

What is more, they don't go around announcing that they are apostles. In fact, there's a very good chance they don't even like this term. And since they aren't part of the latest spiritual fads, you won't find them belonging to any organized church or movement. Nor will you (normally) find them in the Christian tabloids.

While they are less in number than the extravagant and conspicuous "super-apostles" of our time, true workers are making deeper inroads toward God's eternal purpose in Christ. This is because they are building His church in His way.

All of this translates into the following simple prescription: Christians should be *cognizant* of their need for apostolic ministry, *generous* in their support of apostolic workers, yet *cautious* of those claiming to have apostolic status.

CHAPTER 5

THE MODERN HOUSE CHURCH MOVEMENT

*Without a burning vision of the Lord's way, and the
urge of the Spirit to obey, any pattern will remain but
an empty sham.*

—John W. Kennedy

We live in a day where there exists a "primitive church phenomenon."
Countless Christians around the globe are seeing afresh that the
modern practice of "church" is biblically groundless and spiritually
ineffective. As a result, many are leaving the institutional church and
are seeking to return to simpler forms of church life.

Some have dubbed this phenomenon "the house church
movement." But this is a misnomer for two reasons. First, it places
the emphasis on the wrong thing—the house. Granted, the location
of the church meeting is not without significance. But what God is
after goes far beyond where His people meet. To put it bluntly, there

is nothing inherently magical about meeting in a home. While a case can be made that gathering in homes is often superior to gathering in basilicas, it's not the hallmark of the church.

Second, the word *movement* conveys a unified motion among a group of people. The fact is, there are about as many types of house churches as there are varieties of plants. Those who meet in homes contain every stripe of Christian and represent every doctrinal pedigree imaginable. Consequently, there exists no monolithic movement that reflects all house churches. For these reasons, the phrase "house church movement" is misleading. House churches gather for many different reasons and focus on many different things. And these differences are so great that they place many house churches galaxies apart.

While I rejoice that countless believers are pursuing the Lord outside of institutional church structures, it is my conviction that many such churches need guidance in making Christ the center of their church lives.

Subcultures of House Church

According to my experience, most of the groups that fly under the flag of "house church," "simple church," or "New Testament church" fit neatly into one of the following categories:

The Glorified Bible Study. This brand of house church is typically chaired by an ex-clergyman or aspiring Bible teacher. That person usually facilitates a roundtable discussion of the Scriptures. Meetings are dominated by Bible expositions, which often descend into fruitless debates. In the glorified Bible study, those members who are not theologically inclined have a rather thin participation. Whether they recognize it or not, the person facilitating the Bible study is in charge of the church.

The Special Interest Group. These home groups make their focal point of gathering a common interest like homeschool, home birth, the keeping of Jewish feasts, a particular eschatological (end times) view, a *pro forma* pattern of church service, organic farming, personal prophecy, "Holy Ghost laughter," evangelism, or some other issue, fad, or thing—even "house church" itself.

The Institutional Home Church. This is simply a traditional church that meets in a house. A pastor leads it, a church service is followed religiously, a worship leader is in place, etc. The only difference is that the membership is smaller and the gathering place is a home instead of a building. I have a friend who describes such groups by the line "Honey, I shrunk the church!"

The Personality Cult. Members of these groups center their universe around a gifted person. It may be a dead apostle whose writings act as the exclusive medium for the group's identity, beliefs, and practices. More often, the object of attention is a Christian leader who founds the church and perpetually stays resident within it. (Or it's a leader who has welded together a movement to which the church belongs.) While the gifted personality often has a genuine desire to see the body build itself up, his controlling personality obstructs this spiritual dynamic. He is typically blind to the fact that he has unwittingly fostered an unhealthy dependence upon himself. Others can see this quite clearly, except for those who are part of the movement. They are oblivious to it.

The Bless-Me Club. At bottom, this is a narcissistic community—a spiritual ghetto. The meetings are insular and ingrown. The group functions as a spiritual fueling station for burned-out Christians in need of an emotional fix. Churches of this ilk are dominated by navel-gazing individualists. People come together to eat and "hang out" each week. Most meetings are no more than "supperfests."[1]

Jesus Christ is not the centrality of the group, and an understanding of God's eternal purpose is anemic at best. In addition, members typically bail out whenever the group faces a rough thicket. When conflict or dry spells occur, many (including those who were most zealous about the idea of "house church") end up being lured back to the polish and flair of the program-driven traditional church.

The Socially Amorphous Party. These home groups are typically comprised of four to eight people who nebulously meet in a living room to chat over tea and cookies. They rarely attain critical mass due to a lack of vision and purpose. They like to speak bulbously about Jesus being present whenever "two or three are gathered together." However, they usually fold before they even begin to understand why they exist. If they don't fold, their meetings become progressively sterile as the years roll by.

The Disgruntled Malcontent Society. Comprised of ex-church derelicts and recycled Christians, these groups happily assemble to lick their wounds and slam the "spiritually abusive" institutional church. Their meetings are permeated with an atmosphere of pessimism, cynicism, and veiled bitterness. Tragically, after the members tire of attacking the organized church, they begin to chew up one another. Thus they find themselves taken by the same

---

1   In the beginning of an organic church plant, having meals together is recommended. But the church should eventually grow into something more than a weekly supperfest.

spirit they set out to oppose. This form of house church attracts Christians who are deeply wounded and have never learned to trust others.

The Unwritten Liturgy Driven Church. These groups clearly stand outside the stream of traditional Christianity. But they often do not meet in a home. Many gather in a rented building or a "meeting hall." The dominating weakness of their gatherings is the lurking presence of an unwritten liturgy. The ironclad liturgy, which is practiced perfunctorily every week, is never questioned, challenged, or changed. In fact, if the order of worship is broken in any way, the leadership of the church will call the violators on the carpet to reprove them for their irreverence.

The Organic Church. This is a living, vibrant, face-to-face community that has no other pursuit but Jesus Christ Himself. Members are being "built together" into Christ the Head, they are experiencing the cross of Jesus, they are discovering how to live by His indwelling life, and they are fleshing out the biblical vision that the church is the family of God. Such churches are a testimony to the world, to one another, and to principalities and powers that Jesus of Nazareth is indeed alive—alive enough to be Head over His own church. Christ is the church's centrality. He is her passion. He is, as it were, her obsession. Members specialize in nothing—except Christ. Their goal is to make Him visible in their community. Their hallmark is their growing knowledge of the Lord. Their testimony is their openness to all of God's people, their humility, and their unmistakable love for one another. House churches that are not characterized by these spiritual features not only miss a step, but they also dance the wrong dance.

The Short Shelf Life of a House Church

It's quite telling to note that many house churches disintegrate over a brief time span. The average life span is six months to two years.

Within this six-to-two window, the church usually dissolves due to an irreconcilable split or an unresolved crisis. (The crisis is usually rooted in a high-drama power struggle, a sustained bickering over hobbyhorse theology, or an unwillingness to forbear with intractable personalities.)

If the group manages to hold together through the thrall of such conflict, it usually drifts toward a scaled-down, "small is beautiful" version of the institutional church. That is, someone from within the group will devolve into the near equivalent of a modern clergyman.

The other common result is that a group of men who tag themselves "elders" will surface and rule the church in oligarchical fashion—running roughshod over everyone else's sensibilities. In churches of this type, the elders embrace the idea that supervising a church involves breathing down the necks of God's people— controlling the way they dress, vote, eat, and a dozen other things.

Granted, there are house churches that push past the two-year mark—all without clergy or authoritarian elders. Thankfully, such churches are becoming more common in our time. I believe this is partly because we have entered into a new season of the restoration of the church. (More on that later.)

In short, when Jesus Christ is not the center of a noninstitutional church, the only fuel that can drive it is a fascinating issue, a charismatic personality, or a nifty doctrine. But all of these fuels yield low mileage. And when they run dry, the group collapses.

A fellowship of believers can be held together in any beneficial way only when a continual encounter with the Lord Jesus becomes the dominating element. At bottom, if Christ is not the glue of a nontraditional church, its meetings will become shallow, colorless, and eventually unsustainable.

The psalmist once said, "If the foundations be destroyed, what can the righteous do?" (Ps. 11:3 KJV). Why have so many house churches gone belly up? Most often it's because they were not founded upon a revelation of the Lord Jesus Christ. Instead, they were founded upon something less. Either that, or they ended up straying from the centrality of Christ and substituting something else in His place.

Misguided Rallying Points

There are a host of things today that Christians assemble around—even noble things that have something to do with Christ. Doctrines, practices, and viewpoints have taken center stage in many contemporary house churches in the West. Examples would be homeschooling, home birthing, a particular political viewpoint or end-time theology, etc. The list is endless.

These kinds of things hold such groups together. But there is a colossal difference between meeting around some *thing* about the Lord and meeting around the Lord Himself. There is a vast ocean between meeting around an *it* and meeting around *Him*.

If you were to read your New Testament with an eye for discovering how the early churches were formed, you would find that they were solidly built upon an unshakable revelation of Jesus Christ (Matt. 16:16–18). All the churches that Paul planted were built upon this revelation (1 Cor. 3:11). And out of this mighty unveiling of Christ, churches spontaneously issued forth.

It's important to note that the apostolic declaration of Jesus Christ has community-forming properties. According to Scripture, the church is built by the preaching of the Word of God. But that preaching must stop once the foundation has been laid. And then it should resume periodically.

Too much preaching from an apostle (or any person for that matter) will kill church life. Too little will also end up hurting it. The itinerant ministry of church planters is very powerful. If carried out properly, it doesn't overlord because it's not present very often. Yet it's important for a church's proper foundation and its continued progress in the Lord. In this regard, planting a church is like holding a dove in one's hand. If the church planter holds it too tightly, he will kill it. But if he holds it too loosely, it will fly away and be lost.

When a church is founded upon the Lord Jesus Christ, it can survive intense pressure and testing (1 Cor. 3:6–15). The winds may blow brutally and the floods fall fiercely, but the house will stand because it was founded upon a Rock (Matt. 7:24–27; Luke 6:46–48). Put another way, Jesus Christ and His cross are the only unmovable foundations upon which God's people may rightfully gather. By "His cross," I don't only mean His redemptive work, but also the experience of dying to oneself. The church exists because of Calvary. But it lives and survives when God's people bear the cross and die to themselves (Matt. 16:24–25; Mark 8:34–35; Luke 14:27; 1 Cor. 15:31; 2 Cor. 4:11–12).

Therefore, those Christians who are seeking to experience church life without the sturdy props of human hierarchy must build their community upon the Lord Jesus Christ and His cross. If they do not, their chances of surviving are pretty low. While having healthy apostolic input is no guarantee for the longevity of a church, it's an important help.

The First Wave of House Church

In the late 1960s and early 1970s, the United States saw its first move of God outside the religious system. Countless converts were made during this time period. Many of them began to meet in the primitive simplicity of homes without a clergy. Most of these budding "churches" were populated with young people.

A number of clerical leaders felt it was their responsibility to bring stability to the growing movement. Many of these men left their clerical positions on Sunday and instantly rose to become leaders of the new movement on Monday.

In a very short time span, these men introduced to these simple and innocent groups a form of discipleship that eventually squeezed out all semblance of life. While their motives were noble, they did untold damage to a genuine move of God. The young converts who once knew no human headship were used to spawn international movements (some of which eventually became full-fledged denominations). Those movements were built on legalism and authoritarianism. These movements swallowed up scores of living, breathing organic churches and Christian communities. Christian lives were shipwrecked on the rock of a perverted doctrine of authority. The work of God was choked by the hands of men.

How could this happen? Very simply: These leaders knew nothing of God's way of raising up workers. They had never spent a day in organic church life as nonleaders. Though they were gifted, they were neither prepared nor sent.

The Second Wave of House Church

During the late 1980s and early 1990s, the United States witnessed its second stirring outside the traditional church. It was at this time that the phrase "house church movement" was born. Unlike the earlier move of God, most of the people in the second wave were not youth, but middle-aged adults. Few of them were new converts. Most were Christians who were disaffected with the institutional church. In fact, many of them became Christians during the first wave. So they left their sacred buildings, they dumped their pastors, and they began gathering in homes.

As a reaction to the flaws of the first movement, the second wave of house church folk looked upon any form of itinerant church planting with a suspicious eye. The movement was taken captive by a spirit of absolute egalitarianism that ruled out any need for extralocal help. *Leadership* became a dirty word, and "leaders" were viewed in the worst possible light.

The peril of the first "house church movement" was the fact that God's people didn't exercise discernment in welcoming itinerant ministry. They embraced a group of spiritual leaders who were untested and untrained (biblically speaking). None of them spent any time being prepared within the context of an existing organic church. Instead, these people retained their clerical statuses. They simply switched their sphere of ministry from the basilica to the home. Interestingly, the letter of 2 John speaks to this very problem. In it, John warns a local assembly not to receive untested workers (vv. 10–11).

Regrettably, the second "house church movement" was plagued by the opposite problem. It failed to receive those whom God had genuinely sent. Interestingly enough, the message of 3 John addresses this very issue. John makes mention of Diotrephes, who would not receive the traveling workers whom John sent to minister to the churches (vv. 1–11).

A New Wave

Today, a third wave of organic church is upon us. A "revolution" as George Barna and others are calling it.[2]

Every year, one million adults leave the institutional church in the United States. According to missional church expert Reggie McNeal, "A growing number of people are leaving the institutional church for a new reason. They are not leaving because they have lost their faith. They are leaving the church to preserve their faith."

We are living in a day of new beginnings. It's a new season for the restoration of God's house. God is breaking new ground with respect to the shape, the mission, and the practice of the church. Many Christians are longing for the organic expression of the church—for this is what their spiritual instincts cry out for. Organic church life is our native habitat—it's our natural environment. The groundswell in the body of Christ for such is increasing.

It's crucial, therefore, that we do not repeat the mistakes of the past—on either end. May the Lord give us open hearts as well as spiritual discernment so that the Lord Jesus may be given first place in these new expressions of church.

---

2   For details see "The Current Move of God: Eight Characteristics" at www.ptmin.org/currentmove. pdf.

CHAPTER 6

RESTORATION OR REVOLUTION?

It has often been that the greatest thing of God has been very small in the eyes of man.

—T. Austin-Sparks

In the latter part of the twentieth century, there was a small surplus of books written on the restoration of the apostolic ministry. Many of these books claimed that the 1990s would be "the decade of the apostle." They asserted with absolute certainty that God would raise up "thousands of apostles," restoring the apostolic ministry to the body of Christ on a grand scale.

The '90s have passed us by, and none of these high claims have come to pass. Nevertheless, some of these authors continue to carry on quite loudly about the "restoration" of the apostle and the other "fivefold ministry" gifts at some nebulous date in the future.

Interestingly, this same "prediction" has been with us since 1948.[1] The literature, claims, exact rhetoric, and "prophecies" that were put to pen in that year are identical to what is being said today.

Some have called the movement that emphasizes the restoration of ministry gifts "the Restoration Movement." It's my opinion that this movement has been tried and found wanting. What is needed in the body of Christ is not restoration. It's not even revival.[2] What is needed is a *revolution*—a complete and radical change from top to bottom, a new sighting of Jesus Christ and His church, and a change of both mind-set and practice.

To put it bluntly, we need a revolution in our understanding of the Christian life. We need a revolution in our practice of the church. And we need a revolution in our approach to church planting. Consider the following table that isolates the key differences between *restoration* and *revolution:*

---

1   While the Restoration Movement has antecedents elsewhere during the nineteenth century, it picked up steam during the "Latter Rain Movement" in Canada in the late 1940s. See my article "Rethinking the Fivefold Ministry" for details: www.ptmin.org/fivefold.htm.

2   Historically, revivals resurrect a dying church back to ground zero. Once the church is resurrected and the revival ends, the church continues on with the same unscriptural practices it had before it sank into death. Revival, therefore, is merely a temporary solution to a long-term problem.

RESTORATION	REVOLUTION
1919: "Apostles" are seen as wielding official authority over pastors and congregations. They typically engender fan-club followings, are treated like celebrities, and happily sport the title "apostle."	"Apostles" are largely hidden and broken vessels who sport no titles. They hold no office. Like Paul of Tarsus, they usually work for a living.[3] Most have a distaste for the word *apostle* and never use it to describe themselves.[4]
Emphasizes the victorious living of the individual Christian.	Emphasizes the corporate life and Christ-centered experience of the believing community.
Emphasizes "spiritual gifts," "power," "signs and wonders."	Emphasizes the eternal purpose of God, the deeper work of the cross, and the centrality of Jesus Christ.
Measures success by large conferences that draw thousands and the number of churches that are part of their "movement."	Measures success by quality; ignores the size of the crowd. (Throughout Paul's entire ministry, he planted only around fourteen churches. Paul was more concerned with *quality* than *quantity*.)
Stresses the spectacular things of what God is "going to do" in the *future*.	Stresses the unsearchable riches that are available in Christ *now* and shows God's people how to appropriate them *today*.
Focuses on spiritual warfare and triumphing over the Devil. (The Devil gets almost as much airplay as does the Lord.)	Focuses on the glories of Jesus Christ. The Devil is viewed as defeated and is largely ignored.
Churches are controlled by pastors, high-powered apostles, or all-powerful elders who do virtually all the spoken ministry.	Churches are led by *all* the brothers and sisters in Christ. Members have been equipped to function and care for the church by extralocal workers who leave them on their own.
Much talk about "equipping the saints" where they will be ready to minister in some elusive date in the future.	"Equipping the saints" is not a buzzword, but a reality. God's people minister *now* in the meetings of the church and to the lost.
Sees the church as a fighting army. But in reality it's an institution that requires a church building, a pastor, and a Sunday-morning order of worship.	Sees the church as a free-flowing, beautiful woman—a new species, "the third race" that's inseparable from Jesus Christ Himself. The sacred church building, the modern pastoral office, and the Sunday-morning liturgy have all been abandoned.
Embraces an old, tiresome mind-set that's rooted in Western individualism and seventeen hundred years of ecclesiastical tradition.	Embraces an entirely new mind-set that's rooted in the New Testament narrative and the fellowship of the Godhead.

3   An apostle has a right to receive full financial support from the churches he works with (not a salary, but financial help). Paul, however, did not exercise this right (2 Thess. 3:8–9; 1 Cor. 9:3–12; 2 Cor. 11:8–9; 12:14).

4   The reason for this is because the term *apostle* has become corrupted, abused, and filled with an ego-inflated, unbiblical meaning.

PART TWO
TILLING THE GROUND—
ANSWERS TO QUESTIONS

CHAPTER 7

CAN THE NEW TESTAMENT EXAMPLE BE APPLIED TODAY?

Objection: Conditions are very different today in the Western world than they were in the first century. Back then, the entire world was unsaved. There was no institutional church. Church planters like Paul did not take born-again Christians from traditional churches and teach them how to meet New Testament–style. Modern church planters, therefore, cannot point to Paul as an example of what they do.

Granted, the apostolic mission of the first century was one of pioneer evangelism into virgin territory. The gospel of Jesus Christ was brand new. There was no institutional church. Thus the bulk of Paul's converts fell into two categories: (1) those who came straight out of the pagan pool, and (2) God-fearing Gentiles who were institutionalized by the Jewish synagogues. Both were "virgin soil" situations.

But Paul's mission had two objectives. First, it was to convert lost souls. The second objective was interconnected with the first. It was to form local communities that bore corporate testimony to the kingdom of God. We have sadly reversed this order today. We have made the saving of lost souls the goal of the church when the opposite is true. The goal of saving souls was to build the *ekklesia* so that God may have a bride, a house, a family, and a body. This is His ultimate purpose.[1]

The contemporary practice of saving souls outside the context of the church of Jesus Christ is foreign to the Bible. The first-century Christians had no such concept. For them, being saved meant being added to the local community of believers. And being added to the local community of believers meant being saved. The two were inseparable. This is why the New Testament says that to be added to the church was to be added to the Lord and vice versa (Acts 5:14; 11:24 NKJV).

Put another way, Paul's chief goal in preaching the gospel was to create Spirit-baptized communities that corporately expressed the Lord Jesus Christ on earth. Consider the following:

> *The New Testament does not offer much support to evangelistic strategies that concentrate merely on the converting of individuals. (Stuart Murray)[2]*

> *Paul, unlike the field preachers, did not primarily deliver an individualistic challenge to give up vice*

---

1   See my book *From Eternity to Here* for details.

2   Stuart Murray, *Church Planting: Laying Foundations* (Scottdale, PA: Herald, 2001), 71.

but aimed at forming a community with those who responded to his proclamation. (Abraham Malherbe)[3]

From what has already been said it is manifest that St. Paul did not go about as a missionary preacher merely to convert individuals: he went to establish churches from which the light might radiate throughout the whole country round. (Roland Allen)[4]

The only exception in the entire New Testament that records a case of individual salvation is that of Philip leading the Ethiopian eunuch to the Lord (Acts 8:26ff.). Everywhere else, people were saved into the community of the believers.

To put it in a sentence, Paul's missional impulse was not the saving of lost souls. Nor was it to relieve human suffering or poverty. Rather, it was to create Christian communities that fulfilled God's ageless purpose. Out of the life of such communities everything else would flow.

Paul formed Christian communities by fathering, mothering, and nursing the Christians with whom he worked (1 Thess. 2:7–12; 1 Cor. 4:15). He showed the church how to fellowship with its Lord, how to mature in Christ, how to function in its gatherings, and how to solve specific problems endemic to community life.

Tragically, these are things that many (if not most) Christians in the institutional church know little about. To put it bluntly, being a seasoned Christian does not equip one to be a functioning

---

3   Quoted in Clarence Glad, *Paul and Philodemus* (Leiden, Netherlands: E. J. Brill, 1995), 6.
4   Roland Allen, *Missionary Methods: St. Paul's or Ours?* (Grand Rapids, MI: Eerdmans, 1962), 81.

member in an organic church setting. Nor does it prepare one to be a contributing member of a Christian community. In addition, finding oneself two thousand years into Christian history and five hundred years down the Reformation pike does not prepare one for such a task.

As A. W. Tozer once put it, the modern church "is an asylum for retarded spiritual children." It's a nursery for overgrown spiritual babes, most of whom do not have a clue about how to function spiritually with their fellow brethren in a coordinated way. And why is this? *Because they have never been shown how.* Instead, they have been habituated to stay silent and passive. (Except, of course, when it comes to sharing the gospel with the lost. Preachers have been pounding that into the heads of Christians since the days of D. L. Moody.) God's people, therefore, need to be unleashed and empowered to minister in the house of God.

For this reason, the Pauline ministry of planting churches is still very much needed today. Again, far more goes into building a church than leading people to the Lord. Winning converts is merely a first step. Enriching, equipping, and empowering them to get on with God and with their fellow brethren make up the rest of the trip.

To use Peter's language, to lead a sinner to Christ is to convert a dead stone into a living stone (1 Peter 2:5). But the accumulation of living stones is not God's purpose. Today, we have many living stones on the planet, but they are scattered and isolated. God's goal is for all of those stones to be formed into a house—His very own dwelling place (Eph. 2:22). Therein lies the main calling of the Christian worker (1 Cor. 3:9–10). It's not merely the conversion of dead stones into living stones; it's to *build* the house of the living God with those stones. And that takes far more than simply preaching sermons once or twice a week. It means equipping the people of God to function in the church meetings, to take care of one another, and to witness to the glories of Christ before the world as a close-knit, Christ-centered community.

Consequently, if Paul were in the Western world today, it's extremely likely that he would seek out the lost sheep as well as the isolated sheep. To be sure, Paul would present the gospel to lost souls. But hungry Christians in the traditional church would doubtlessly attach themselves to his work as well. Would Paul refuse to minister to them simply because they were "already" converted? Not a chance.

Paul's goal was a kingdom community. It was a shared-life assembly that lives by divine life and is held together by Jesus Christ and nothing else. So he would undoubtedly minister to all the Christians who were open to him—new converts and institutionalized believers. He would enrich them to know Christ, equip them to express Him corporately, and empower them to function in a coordinated way.

Genuine workers in our day do just that.

Not to put too fine a point on it, Paul's passion was to establish Christian communities marked by every member functioning, and that expressed the fullness of Jesus Christ. It was not to rescue individuals from eternal judgment (though that was included). We can be confident that if Paul were with us today, he would not be hindered from this all-consuming mission.

CHAPTER 8

WAS PAUL AN EXCEPTION?

Objection: The idea of a church being founded by or helped by a traveling worker is a theme found exclusively in Paul's ministry. The churches that weren't associated with Paul did not need extralocal help. In fact, some of those churches were founded without an apostolic worker. Therefore, you are overstating your case when you say that all churches today should have extralocal help.

Since Paul dominates the pages of the New Testament narrative, the principle of extralocal workers founding and subsequently helping a church is most clearly seen in his ministry.

However, if you examine all the churches mentioned in the New Testament (there are over thirty of them),[1] you will discover that

---

1   According to the New Testament, there was a church planted in each of the following cities: Jerusalem, Damascus, Lydda, Joppa, Caesarea, Syrian Antioch, Salamis, New Paphos, Pisidian Antioch, Iconium, Lystra, Derbe, Troas, Philippi, Thessalonica, Berea, Corinth, Cenchrea, Ephesus, Laodicea, Colosse, Hierapolis, Smyrna, Thyatira, Sardis, Philadelphia, Pergamum, Tyre, Ptolemais, Rome, Nicopolis. If you add the churches mentioned in specific regions, the number increases. Again, virtually all of these churches were directly planted by or helped by an itinerant worker. The pattern is consistent.

virtually all of them were either founded by an itinerant worker or helped by one after its birth.

Paul and his company (Barnabas, Silas, Timothy, Titus, Epaphras, etc.) were not the only workers who traveled to plant, strengthen, and recenter churches. Peter, John, and (according to church history) the rest of the Twelve were also sent to the work of building the church—thus the reason why they are called "sent ones" (apostles). Also, the letters of Peter and John were written to churches in their apostolic care.

Some have argued that extralocal workers are an unnecessary artifact because several churches mentioned in the New Testament were not founded by one. People who employ this argument typically point to the churches that were formed during the Jerusalem dispersion. So let us explore again what really happened there.

The twelve apostles founded the Jerusalem church. They laid the foundation for that church for a period of four years. After those four years, the church in Jerusalem dispersed into Judea, Samaria, and Galilee. Some of the believers dispersed into Cyprus. Others journeyed as far as Syria. The Christians who dispersed into these new places began to meet just as they did in Jerusalem. And God added to their number as they naturally and organically shared the gospel with the lost.

As we have already seen in chapter 1, the church in Jerusalem was *transplanted* into these other regions. In Acts 9:31 (NASB), Luke tells us that the church (singular) found rest in Judea, Galilee, and Samaria. In other words, the church in Jerusalem simply relocated to these different regions.

Keep in mind that the brethren who were part of these transplanted churches had (1) been initially helped by the twelve apostles for a period of four years, and (2) experienced the corporate life of the church in Jerusalem during those years.

In other words, the Jerusalem Christians transplanted their *experience* of church life that they received from the help of the apostles. They didn't leave the synagogues one day and start new churches the next.

More important, after these newly transplanted churches were formed, they were subsequently helped by the apostles. The Twelve itinerantly circulated among the new churches (much like Paul's practice) and ministered to them (Acts 8—12). This point is often overlooked.

Along this line, the modern idea that an organic church should multiply rapidly shortly after its birth sounds great on paper, but there are three problems with it. First, it takes a lot of time for a proper foundation to be laid for an organic church, where the members have been equipped to know Jesus Christ in the depths and to survive together for the long haul. Second, most groups that multiply quickly disintegrate just as quickly. And before they do, they are profoundly shallow. The reason is because there wasn't enough time given for the group to grow roots. Third, rapid multiplication cannot be supported by the New Testament narrative. The church in Jerusalem didn't multiply until it had four years of intense ministry from the apostles and a daily experience of face-to-face community.

Those who push for rapid multiplication seem more interested in using the church as a technique for evangelism rather than as the corporate expression of Jesus Christ that stands for God's ageless purpose. And in my observation, the former is not a very effective means for evangelism in the first place. It's a mistake to send babies out into the world right after they are born into a family. Better to wait until they are adults before they relocate to another place to begin a new family.

In short, the independent house church that rejects the help of itinerant workers shares one common feature with the institutional, clergy-led church. They both have no analog in the New Testament.

CHAPTER 9

IS CHURCH PLANTING ELITIST?

Objection: The idea of an extralocal worker is an elitist notion. It elevates one person above everyone else. It creates a separate elitist class set apart to instruct "ordinary" believers. It's no different from the clergy that drives the institutional church. We Christians are the priesthood of God. All we need is Jesus! We don't need a man to help us. And we certainly don't need any "superstar" church planters to tell us what we already know. In fact, it is dangerous to have a church planter, because you are following a man instead of God.

The main problem with this argument is that it rejects a God-given ministry to the body of Christ under the guise of "protecting" the priesthood of believers. In philosophy, this is called a straw-man argument. It unfairly paints all workers as elitist people. Then it effectively argues against this image by hiding behind the pious rhetoric of "just needing Jesus and not a man."

Indeed, there are false apostles who seek to fleece the sheep. There are untested and unsafe workers—control freaks, if you will—who lord over God's people. And there are church planters who are sectarian, elitist, and egotistical.

Consequently, if a Christian worker believes that he and the workers who are involved in his movement are the only authentic workers on the planet, my advice is to head for the door. That's elitism in spades. By the same token, if a worker believes that only the churches that he plants are legitimate, he is sectarian and egotistical—if not delusional. So again, head for the door or jump out of a window if you have to!

But to paint all workers this way is patently unfair and inaccurate. I am friends with numerous Christian workers who are honest, genuine, and safe to God's people. Each of them has a different emphasis and gifting, but all are being used to build the kingdom of God.

Even so, if we apply the above objection to the New Testament narrative, the fallacy emerges in bold relief. Apply this logic to the Bible, and we would have to conclude the following: that Paul, Barnabas, Silas, Timothy, Titus, Epaphras, and every other person who planted churches in the first century were "superstar" Christians who belonged to a "separate elitist class" set apart to instruct the poor "ordinary" believers.

We would have to also conclude that ...

The churches in Galatia, Greece, and Asia Minor should have boldly told Paul, Barnabas, Silas, Timothy, and Epaphras, "We don't need you. You are mere men. We just need Jesus. You guys will harm the priesthood of all believers."

If you buy into the mentality of "away with church planters, we just need Jesus," you are unwittingly saying, "Away with the Twelve, away with Paul, away with Barnabas, away with Silas, and away with Timothy."

In addition, the idea that the church doesn't need a human being to assist it cannot be reconciled with the record of the early church. When Jesus Christ walked this earth in flesh and blood, one could rightly say, "We don't need anyone but Jesus."

But since He ascended and poured forth His Spirit, Jesus Christ has chosen to use women and men to accomplish His mission on earth. The Lord uses fallen people—flesh and blood—to preach the gospel, to plant and nurture churches. He uses fallen but redeemed humans to make disciples and instruct new converts. He uses people to train and equip local fellowships.

So no matter how you slice it, God has chosen to use human beings.

Therefore, those who would push the "we do not need men, we need only Jesus" envelope contradict New Testament revelation.

To be sure, God's people need to be cautious of false apostles who seek to take advantage of them. But if we are serious about moving toward spiritual fullness, we will discerningly welcome the contributions of all whom God has placed in His body—including the role that itinerant workers play.

Itinerant workers, if they are the genuine articles, are not spiritual elitists. They do not have a different status from other Christians. Instead, they are ordinary, and very imperfect, Christians like everyone else. Only with a different calling.

They do not run local churches nor are they distant bosses over them. God is the only boss. Workers are simply servants to the churches they help. Their ties with the believers they work with are familial and relational, not official or hierarchical.

The fact is, some people in the body of Christ have a gift for spotting and engaging the whole range of gifts and insights that a church is letting lie fallow. They have a talent for graciously redressing a church's weaknesses and keeping it from being distracted by those things that will sap its energy. They also have a knack for getting the church to walk through those difficult minefields that are necessary for making progress in the war of love.

Workers do not accomplish these things by pulpiteering or pontificating. Instead, they patiently and relentlessly minister, counsel, sit and talk, listen, coddle, encourage, empathize, and do everything else they can think of to get God's people to look past the foibles of others and discover that they really can walk together as brothers and sisters.

Workers are like catalysts in chemical reactions. They have a gift for galvanizing and catalyzing action among the rest of the body of Christ. They inject fresh life into the church when its pulse begins to wane. They keep foreign elements out so the church can grow naturally. They prevent the ambitious from controlling the church and drawing it after a strong personality. They recenter the believers on Christ when their eyes begin to move away from Him to lesser things. They rebuild, reshape, redirect, and edify God's people, and then they leave. Consequently, as with all the gifts in the body of Christ, their contribution is important.

Without a doubt, some people become antagonistic when the subject of church planting comes up. The emotionally laden and highly flammable reactions to the mere mention of it suggest that a nerve is being probed somewhere. It's nearly impossible to sort through the assortment of motivations that lie behind these reactions. But let's unearth the more common ones.

For some, the sore spot is the result of a bad experience with a Christian worker who has left them bitter and reactionary. So now they lump all workers into the same contaminated camp. To use Gotthold Lessing's unfortunate phrase, untrustable workers, just like modern CEO pastors, are the "accidental truths of history." And historical accidents ought never to be taken as the norm by which to judge all spiritual leadership.

Another reason for the backlash against extralocal help has its roots in certain abuses that took place during the Jesus Movement in the early 1970s. Some have responded to these abuses by championing the cause of "anti-leadership."

Regrettably, many of God's people have suffered under authoritarian leadership models. Yet those who have moved to the opposite extreme and wave the "anti-leadership" flag perpetuate their own brand of oppression.

"Anti-leadership" has the net effect of gutting all leadership language out of the New Testament. It deludes itself into believing that by "taking a stand" against leaders, we have accomplished something righteous and noble.

Some "anti-leaders" are active and bellicose, chafing against all who have an influence in the lives of God's people. Others are passive-aggressives who have the remarkable ability to stalemate any church by insisting that no one ever lead anything.

This typically results in a church "led" manipulatively and subversively by the person who refuses to let others lead. And by and large, the "second state is worse than the first."

On the darker side, there is something lurking within some people's hearts that objects to receiving help from others. Such individuals mask the real reason for their opposition by vilifying those who plant churches. (If you listen to their half-clear ravings carefully enough, the real motive will eventually slip out of their mouths.)

There is a gentleman mentioned in the New Testament who refused to receive the workers whom John the apostle sent to strengthen the churches in his care (3 John 5–11). John laid bare the dark motive that lay behind this person's rejection of God-sent workers. It was because he "loved to have the preeminence" in the church.

This man very well may have concealed his desire for prominence by hiding behind the "we do not need these workers, we just need Jesus" platitude. But underneath these words he was really saying, "I do not want anyone to follow the ministry of *another* person. I am afraid of losing *my* place of influence and prominence in the eyes of the church. I want the members to look to *me* for direction instead of someone else." In my experience, those who claim that the church does not need any kind of leadership are those who wish to be leaders themselves.

The irony here is that one of the roles of an extralocal worker is to protect the church from those local brethren suffering from *apostleitis*, clamoring for the attention of God's people. *Apostleitis* is the unrealistic desire to become an apostle. Those who suffer from this disease have no idea what the apostolic call involves, for if they did, they would never pursue it. The disease typically afflicts ambitious young men who aspire to be apostles. These men are either control freaks or dreamers who are out of touch with reality. The apostolic calling is a death sentence. It's one of the worst things to befall an individual (1 Cor. 4:9–13; 2 Cor. 1:8–10; 4:1–12; 6:3–10; 11:1—12:10).

In his book *Lost in the Cosmos*, Walker Percy summarizes the human problem by pressing the following questions: Are you in trouble? If you are, have you sought help? If help came, did you accept it?

Percy makes the penetrating observation that many modern folk are in trouble but do not know it. They have never bothered to seek help. And they would not accept it if it came. This point warrants sober reflection. Those who have left the traditional church are ripe to seek the Lord in humility about this issue. It's high time we swallow our initial reactions and confront and subdue our bitterness, prejudice, and theories, asking God to give us light—and if necessary, healing.

In a nutshell, a worker's task is to work himself out of a job. A Christian worker's ministry thrives in a spiritual culture that appreciates leadership without deifying it. Contemporary workers, like Paul, play visible roles in the births and ongoing lives of the churches they found. You can find that in Robert Banks if you're looking for a footnote.[1]

---

1   "Church Order and Government" in *Dictionary of Paul and His Letters* (Downers Grove, IL: InterVarsity, 1993), 136.

CHAPTER 10

CAN'T ANYONE START AN ORGANIC CHURCH?

Objection: Anyone can start a church. You don't need to wait passively for a church planter to help you do this. I have several children. I didn't have any experience in raising kids before this. But I learned on the job. I didn't need another person to help me give birth to my babies or raise them. Therefore, I don't need a person to show me how to start a church. I can just start one. And so can everyone else.

I have some good friends in the house church movement who teach that planting a church is as easy as baking a cake. Add water and stir, microwave on high for two minutes, and voilà, a bona fide *ekklesia* is born.

And ... anyone can do it.

Do I agree with this idea? Well, it depends. In one sense, yes. In another sense, no.

Through the years, I've learned that when people have a disagreement over a particular issue, sometimes the disagreement is rooted in a semantic problem. The definitions and paradigms that are used are drastically different. To put it in proverb form: *When two seemingly valid ideas are in disagreement, draw a distinction.*

I believe that some of the disagreements concerning church planting are a case of the latter. If so, reframing the question in order to draw out a distinction may resolve the disagreement.

That said, I propose that we step back from the question of who can plant a church and ask a more basic question: "What *kind* of church are we talking about planting in the first place?"

For instance: If what we mean by "church" is a group of Christians who meet in a home once a week, share a meal, drink java and eat cookies, sing some songs, pray, and have Bible study, then I would agree with those who say that virtually any Christian can start such a church.

In spiritual things, you can only duplicate those things you have experienced. If you've experienced salvation, for example, then you can lead others into the experience of salvation. If you've experienced prayer, then you can teach others how to pray, etc.

Repeat: If your view of "church" is simply meeting in a home once a week to have a shared meal, some prayer, some singing, and some Bible study, then I would say that most Christians can start such a church. Why? Because most Christians have experienced these things.

But suppose that one's view of "church" is something different from the above. Suppose that what we mean by "church" is a group of Christians who are living as a shared-life community under the headship of Jesus Christ.

Suppose that this kind of church is a gathered community that's having an ongoing encounter and experience of Jesus Christ together.

This community gathers often, not just once a week. And when the members gather, no human being is leading or facilitating. In other words, there is no pastor, no reverend, and no minister—whether titled or untitled. Instead, the members are gathering under Christ's headship alone.

As to their meetings, they are not a Bible study, a prayer meeting, a songfest, or a supperfest, but something different. Namely, the church meets to reveal and display Jesus Christ together out of a real, experiential, life-giving encounter with the Lord. And everyone is functioning on equal footing. No one is dominating. And few, if any, are passive.

This is a church where the members are learning to live by divine life together, and they are finding creative ways to express that life week after week, month after month, and year after year. They are living for God's grand mission—incarnating His eternal purpose in the world.

The members of the church see themselves as sisters and brothers. And they pursue the Lord throughout the week, not only individually, but also corporately. In addition, they live their lives together as a family. They take care of one another. They don't just talk about community; they experience it in living color.

The church also makes decisions by consensus. They have no pastor or elite group of men who rule over or control them. Direction comes from the entire body together. The members have learned to function in a coordinated way.

Also, they handle their own problems as they come up. (Incidentally, when a group of Christians meets once a week for a Bible study, songfest, or supperfest, they will experience minimal problems. But when they live in authentic community, the problems are endless.)

With that said, let me rephrase our original question. *Can anyone plant the sort of church that I've described in the last few paragraphs? And can they do it without imposing rules and laws on God's people? In addition, can they leave the church on its own—without human headship—once they've laid the foundation?*

The answer is clearly no.

And the witness of the New Testament agrees.

According to the biblical record, God has called, equipped, and gifted certain members of the body of Christ to raise up—and help sustain—this kind of church life.

The last twenty-one years of my experience confirm this as well.[1]

In short, I have reframed the issue of who can plant a house church as a relative one rather than a black and white one where some stand on one side of the fence ("anyone can plant a church") and others stand on the other side ("only certain people can plant churches").

The issue is indeed not a black and white one. It's a matter of seeing different shades of gray. Nor is it an issue of defining a valid church against an invalid one—a superior one to an inferior one. It's a matter of *expression*. Therefore, the difference between my friends and me is a relative one. Hopefully over time, this difference will shake itself out.

---

1   Note that I have seen organic churches come into being spontaneously without anyone starting them. However, in virtually every case, that beautiful experience dies rather quickly—typically between six months and two years. There's one exception. If it receives appropriate apostolic help, its chances of survival are far better.

Paul's great argument in 1 Corinthians 12 and Romans 12 is that not all Christians have the same gift. So we should be very careful about stepping into a gift or calling that God has not given to us. As Paul says,

> God hath set some in the church, first apostles, secondarily prophets, thirdly teachers.... Are all apostles? are all prophets? are all teachers? (1 Cor. 12:28–29 KJV)

Paul's unmistakable answer to these questions is no. Not everyone is called to be apostles or prophets or teachers. God has gifted His people with different gifts and functions. And that includes those who are "sent" to plant and nurture churches from the outside.

Therefore, the logic that says "since I can give birth to babies, then I can give birth to a New Testament–styled church" is invalid. Perhaps you can begin a church. And perhaps it will experience organic church life for a time. But organic church life always dies. And when it does, it requires those who know how to resurrect it and keep it alive.

People can escape into theories all day about the help or hindrance of extralocal workers. But the issue really boils down to the kind of church life you are seeking to have. Consider Paul's words:

> If the whole body were an eye, where would the sense of hearing be? If the whole body were an ear, where would the sense of smell be? But in fact God has arranged the parts in the body, every one of them, just as he wanted

them to be. If they were all one part, where would the
body be? (1 Cor. 12:17–19)

What follows are two emails I received from people who were
part of house churches that refused to have any kind of extralocal
help. The first is from a man; the second from a woman:

> *In the beginning of last year, we attempted to start*
> *doing home churching. All the warnings that you stated*
> *in your writings came true. We had a few moments of*
> *glory, but a lot more heartaches. We are all Christians,*
> *and as Christians we are supposed to get along right?*
> *Well.*
>
> *We were 5 families meeting together for about a year.*
> *My wife and I pleaded for outside help from the very*
> *beginning, but the loudest and most prideful brothers*
> *won out. We tried very hard to convince our group*
> *that we needed help, but most folks did not want*
> *outside help.*
>
> *After 12 months the home church is left in ashes, but*
> *prayerfully the Lord will raise up a new church of*
> *people. People who want to learn and be humble.*

I struggle to understand how people could even begin to think they are capable of experiencing the Lord in His fullness, just because locations have moved, without the involvement of a worker/planter. We are so ingrained with our Western mindset and have no concept of the depth of that mentality.

There are enough damaged/disillusioned/hurting/ abused Christians that are hungering to know the Lord that it scares me to think of a bunch of them getting together without really comprehending what it means to die to self, and they end up hurting one another.

You and I both know, it's hard living in church life.... Even though you have spoken about the assumption that exists in the house church movement about any Christian being equipped and called for God's work, there are going to be those who think, "House church. How hard can that be? Why, we've already got some folks who know how to 'do' this. How difficult can it be to learn about Jesus? What do we need a worker for? We're all mature Christians."

You hit the nail on the head in addressing the issue of individualism. We are so steeped in that, even in the church, because most of us are unable or unwilling to count the cost (loss) of knowing Jesus Christ. My heart is

already sad for those who will overlook the importance
of having a church planter from the onset.

I could multiply many more examples of these sorts of letters. In fact, just last week, I received an email from a woman who had been meeting with a house church for the last year. It recently "exploded" (her word), and it wasn't pretty. The reason was that the majority didn't want any kind of outside help. They "knew it all" themselves.

Does this mean that church planters always succeed? Absolutely not. Church planters are just as frail and mortal as everyone else. Again, Peter is a classic example. They have the same foibles, eccentricities, and weaknesses as do other believers. What is more, every organic church will face problems and experience failures. It matters not if they were founded or helped by an itinerant worker.

Virtually all the churches that Paul planted had problems. Just read his epistles.

Consequently, the presence of an itinerant worker will never prevent a church from undergoing problems and failures. But the difference is in how those problems and failures are handled when they arrive. An organic church that rejects extralocal help is totally on its own when it faces a crisis. It's like the proverbial boat that is stuck in the raging sea without oars. Self-correction can go only so far. This is because in virtually every case, those within the group are in some way part of the problem.

When extralocal help is present, however, the church possesses an external resource that knows the church well on the one hand, but isn't part of the problem on the other. These two features, coupled with the worker's spiritual and practical experience, make him an invaluable benefit to a church that's undergoing difficulty.

Many years of wandering around the wilderness might be spared if a church has an experienced resource from the outside who can give it guidance, encouragement, and direction. Such guidance should always be given with a view to equipping the church so that she can eventually build herself up. So while itinerant workers are not a panacea, they are a resource that no church should do without.

CHAPTER 11

WASN'T PAUL THE LAST APOSTLE?

Objection: Didn't Paul say that he was the last apostle? And didn't he say that one of the evidences of an apostle is to see Jesus Christ? Therefore, apostles (church planters) have passed away, right?

Paul never said that he was the last apostle. And there is no New Testament text that states that the ministry of the apostle has passed away.

In 1 Corinthians 15:8–9, Paul said that he was the *least* apostle, not the *last*. He also said that he was the last person to see Jesus Christ physically after about five hundred others saw Him. But Paul never stated that he would be the last person to see the risen Lord. Such assertions are read into the text. They cannot be found in Paul's actual words.

In two of Paul's last letters, he says that God has set in the body of Christ "sent ones," that is, apostles (1 Cor. 12:28; Eph. 4:11). There is no Scripture anywhere that overturns, nullifies, or cancels out those statements. To suggest so is to speak where the Bible has not spoken.

If that is not enough, the last book of the New Testament records the words of Jesus regarding the testing of false apostles. (The mark of a false apostle is one of the following: He seeks money and/or fame, or he supplants the work of other apostles.) If a church must test whether or not a person is a true apostle, this by necessity means that true apostles exist (Rev. 2:2). As Howard Snyder says,

> *Because of the obvious uniqueness of the original apostles, some have argued that apostles no longer exist today. But this conclusion runs counter to the Biblical evidence and makes too sharp a break between the original apostles and the church leaders who followed them.*[1]

What follows is a list of all the apostles mentioned in the New Testament:

Jesus Christ (Heb. 3:1)

The Twelve (Matt. 10:2–4; Mark 3:14–19; Luke 6:13–16):[2]

- ❧ Andrew

- ❧ Bartholomew (also called Nathanael)

- ❧ James, son of Zebedee

- ❧ James, son of Alphaeus

- ❧ John

- ❧ Judas Iscariot (Matthias took his place—Acts 1:26)

---

1   Howard Snyder, *The Community of the King* (Downers Grove, IL: InterVarsity, 1977), 87.

2   The Twelve have special prominence that's not shared with any other apostle who followed them (Matt. 19:28; Rev. 21:14).

- Judas (also called Lebbaeus and surnamed Thaddaeus)

- Matthew (also called Levi)

- Peter (also called Simon)

- Philip

- Simon Zelotes (also called Simon the Canaanite)

- Thomas (also called Didymus)

In addition to the Twelve, the following are also called "apostles" (*apostolos* in Greek):

- Apollos (1 Cor. 4:6–9)

- Andronicus (Rom. 16:7)

- Barnabas (Acts 14:3–4, 14; 1 Cor. 9:5–6)

- Epaphroditus (Phil. 2:25)

- James, the Lord's brother (1 Cor. 15:7; Gal. 1:19)

- Junia (Rom. 16:7)[3]

- Paul (Gal. 1:1; Eph. 1:1; Col. 1:1, et al.)

---

3   All the evidence points to Junia being a woman apostle. That is how the early church fathers interpreted this passage. In fact, no commentator until the twelfth century understood the name to be masculine (see Robert Banks, *Paul's Idea of Community* [Peabody, MA: Hendrickson, 1994], 155; Charles Trombley, *Who Said Women Can't Teach?* [South Plainfield, NJ: Bridge, 1985], 190–91). See also Eldon Jay Epp, *Junia: The First Woman Apostle* (Minneapolis, MN: Fortress, 2005); and F. F. Bruce, *The Pauline Circle* (Grand Rapids, MI: Eerdmans, 1985), 83. Bruce writes of Andronicus and Junia, "Jewish believers whose faith in Christ antedated Paul's. 'They are of note among the apostles,' Paul adds (Rom. 16:7), meaning that they were not only known to the apostles but eminent apostles themselves."

- Silas (1 Thess. 1:1; 2:6)

- Timothy (1 Thess. 1:1; 2:6)

- Titus (2 Cor. 8:23)

Clearly, the New Testament makes evident that Paul was not the last apostle. In addition, the idea that an apostle must physically see Jesus has no support from the New Testament either. Some have pointed to 1 Corinthians 9:1 where Paul asks, "Have I not seen Jesus our Lord?" to prove that apostles must physically see the risen Lord. But Paul was not stating that an apostle must see Christ. He made that statement along with this one: "Am I not free?" Freedom is not a unique qualification for being an apostle. All Christians are free in Christ, not just apostles.

If you continue to read the passage, Paul argues that his apostleship is evidenced by the fruit of his labors—"are you not ... my work in the Lord?"—rather than his being free or having seen the Lord Jesus. While it's true that all twelve apostles saw the resurrected Christ physically (including Matthias), it is not true for many of the other apostles who came after the Twelve. Nevertheless, what is true for all Christian workers is that each of them shares a deep and living revelation of Jesus Christ (Gal. 1:16; 1 Cor. 2:7ff.; Phil. 3:10). For upon that revelation the church is built (Matt. 16:16–18; 1 Cor. 3:11).

CHAPTER 12

DON'T APOSTLES PERFORM SIGNS AND WONDERS?

Objection: Didn't Paul say that signs and wonders are the marks of a true apostle? Therefore, if someone claims to be a church planter, but does not perform signs and wonders, doesn't this mean that he or she is not a true apostle?

The idea that signs and wonders mark an apostle's ministry has been heavily promoted since the turn of the twentieth century. It was during that time that a movement was spawned which gave birth to a particular mind-set. That mind-set placed great value on signs and wonders. The above objection reflects that mind-set.

When Paul's apostleship was under attack, he responded with the one true proof of apostleship. According to Paul, the greatest evidence of an apostle is the founding of an organic church that's given a birth in glory (1 Cor. 9:1–2; 2 Cor. 3:1–3; 13:3–6). In 2 Corinthians 12:12 (NASB), Paul lists other evidences of an apostle:

The signs of a true apostle were performed among you with
all perseverance, by signs and wonders and miracles.

This verse has been translated as follows:

The things which are the characteristic hallmarks of
any apostle happened among you. You saw me live a life
in which again and again I passed the breaking-point
and did not break, a life marked by demonstrations of
the power of God in action, by wonders and miracles.

According to this passage, the signs of an apostolic worker can
be distilled down to two elements: spiritual power and miraculous
power. At the top of Paul's list of apostolic qualifications is the
hallmark of spiritual power: *perseverance.*

The Greek word translated "perseverance" (and "patience" in other
translations) is *hupomone.* It means the ability to abide under pressure.
It's to pass through the breaking point without being broken. It's the
characteristic of a person who is not swerved from his or her purpose
by even the greatest trials and sufferings. Watchman Nee elaborates,

The signs of an apostle will never be lacking where there is
truly an apostolic call.... Endurance is the greatest proof
of spiritual power, and it is one of the signs of an apostle.
It is the ability to endure steadfastly under continuous
pressure that tests the reality of an apostolic call.[1]

---
1   Watchman Nee, *The Normal Christian Church Life* (Anaheim, CA: Living Stream Ministry, 1980),
17.

Apostles are unstoppable creatures. They can be stapled, mutilated, bent, stomped on, rolled over, and yet they will get up, and with their garments still smoking, they'll keep moving forward.

The only way to stop a genuine apostle is to kill him!

Paul's words to the Ephesian elders capture his relentless ambition to endure to the end and finish the race that God called him to run. His words give us insight into his incredible perseverance:

> *I only know that in every city the Holy Spirit warns*
> *me that prison and hardships are facing me. However,*
> *I consider my life worth nothing to me, if only I may*
> *finish the race and complete the task the Lord Jesus has*
> *given me—the task of testifying to the gospel of God's*
> *grace. (Acts 20:23–24)*[2]

Miraculous power is another sign of an apostle. Miraculous power is God's ability to change situations in the physical realm. First-century apostles laid hold of God's power in the face of impending situations that challenged the Lord and His name. The apostle would pray for the sick at times. And he would effect the Holy Spirit's power in high-pressure situations.

But miraculous power is all too often misunderstood today. Surprisingly, out of all the apostles mentioned in the New Testament,

---

2   See also Paul's catalog of sufferings that he endured in 2 Cor. 11:23ff.

only three are recorded as having performed signs and wonders: Jesus, Peter, and Paul.[3]

In Paul's ministry alone, miracles are recorded in only eight towns: Paphos, Iconium, Lystra, Philippi, Corinth, Ephesus, Troas, and Malta.[4] It's an invalid assumption, therefore, to conclude that Paul performed miracles everywhere he went. As Roland Allen explains,

> *Thus it would appear that the importance of miracles in the work of St. Paul may be easily exaggerated. They were not a necessary part of his mission preaching: nor was their influence in attracting converts as great as we often suppose ... their [miracles'] importance can be easily overrated and it is manifest that St. Paul saw this danger and combated it. He does not give the gift of miracles the highest place amongst the gifts of the Spirit. He does not speak as if the best of his workers possessed it. It was not the power of working miracles which was of importance in his eyes: it was the Spirit which inspired the life.*[5]

So the miraculous will be present in the ministry of the modern church planter, but only at those times when it's necessary according to the mind and will of God.

---

3   Barnabas is said to have performed miracles along *with* Paul (Acts 14:3; 15:12). There are only two nonapostles who are recorded as having performed signs and wonders: Stephen (Acts 6:8) and Philip (Acts 8:6). Acts 2:43 and 5:12 are the only places where "the apostles" (plural) are said to have performed signs and wonders. In Rom. 15:18–19, Paul gives general testimony that he performed signs and wonders in his travels from Jerusalem to Illyricum. But he does not say or imply that he performed them in every city that he visited.

4   Acts 13:6–12; 14:3, 8–10; 16:18; 19:11–12; 20:9–12; 28:3–9; 2 Cor. 12:12.

5   Roland Allen, *Missionary Methods: St. Paul's or Ours?* (Grand Rapids, MI: Eerdmans, 1962), 42, 47.

PART THREE
CULTIVATING THE SOIL—PRACTICAL STEPS FOR BEGINNING

CHAPTER 13

DISCOVERING ORGANIC CHURCH

The real trouble is not in fact that the Church is too rich, but that it has become heavily institutionalized, with a crushing investment in maintenance. It has the characteristics of the dinosaur and the battleship. It is saddled with a plant and programme beyond its means, so that it is absorbed in problems of supply and preoccupied with survival. The inertia of the machine is such that the financial allocations, the legalities, the channels of organization, the attitudes of mind, are all set in the direction of continuing and enhancing the status quo. If one wants to pursue a course which cuts across these channels, then most of one's energies are exhausted before one ever reaches the enemy lines.

—John A. T. Robinson

A few years ago, I attended a national house church conference. While I was there, several people requested private meetings with me. Strikingly, each person asked the same question. It was a question that I've been asked numerous times in letters and emails. Here it is:

> *I've been looking for a church that's experiencing organic church life where I live, but I've found none. I've been to several house church web sites and have visited six or seven of the churches listed. All of them were basically smaller versions of the institutional church. They were either traditional Bible studies or church services in a home where there was an untitled pastor leading. I know I'm not ready to plant a church because the Lord hasn't sent me, and I've never experienced organic church life myself. I can't move to another city to be part of an organic church right now due to personal circumstances. So what can I do?*

Of course, some would say, "Just plant a church in your town. It's as simple as making a peanut butter and jelly sandwich."

But again: *What* kind of church are we talking about?

If we're talking about a mere Bible study, a weekly songfest, or a Friday-night supperfest, then sure, you could probably start such a group yourself. But if your vision of the church is the living, breathing *ekklesia* of God—an authentic community that lives by divine life—well, then that's another story.

However, there is hope for those who can't find an organic church in their town and can't relocate to be part of one in another city.

The Forgotten Ministry of Priscilla and Aquila

As we've already seen, Paul uses two metaphors to describe apostolic ministry in 1 Corinthians 3. One is the metaphor of planting a field. The other is the metaphor of laying a foundation for a building. For this reason, apostles are often called "church planters" and "foundation layers."

The foundation that is laid and the seed that is planted is Jesus Christ. Thus those who are called to apostolic ministry must know Christ well. They must also know how to show others how to know Him well.

Why is this important? Because Jesus Christ is the only foundation for a church. Therefore, a clear revelation of Christ must be presented in order for a healthy organic church to be established. This is how all the churches in the first century were planted. Christ was proclaimed and revealed with power and life (see Acts 13—20; 1 Cor. 3; Matt. 16; Eph. 2).

Again: Apostolic workers don't come out of the womb planting churches. They are called by God, then they are prepared by experiencing the glories and gores of organic church life as nonleaders. Finally, they are sent out to the work of church planting.

Now consider these questions with me.

Is there any work that needs to take place before a foundation is laid for a building?

Is there any work that must take place before seed is properly planted into the ground?

The answer to both questions is a resounding yes.

Before the foundation of a building is laid, site preparation must take place. This preconstruction step includes the following: The soil must be tested. The ground must be cleared of debris. The site must be graded (the high places leveled and the low places raised). Footings must be set in order to hold the foundation. And the building materials must be gathered.

In like manner, before seed is planted in a field, the fallow ground must be broken up. The earth must be tilled, the ground cultivated, and the weeds pulled.

Carrying this over into the spiritual realm, some work must be done *before* an apostle lays a foundation and plants a church.

Priscilla and Aquila did this kind of work.

This dynamic duo were "site preparers" and "ground cultivators" who prepared the way for Paul to plant churches.

For this reason, Paul regarded the couple as "fellow workers" (Rom. 16:3), and the Gentile churches were indebted to them (Rom. 16:4). Although Priscilla and Aquila were not apostles, nor resident pastors, they were an integral part of the work of raising up churches.

With this thought in mind, let's return to our original question. If you desire to have organic church life, yet you cannot relocate, nor are you called, prepared, or sent to plant churches, *then become a Priscilla and Aquila.*

Give yourself to the ministry of "site preparation." And prepare the way for a church planter to lay a proper foundation for a new church so that God's people can be equipped to function under the headship of Jesus and live as a kingdom community.

A large part of the ministry of site preparation is to provide a womb wherein the church of Jesus Christ can be born.

In the kingdom of God, there are "initiators." These are people who are gifted at gathering others together. They initiate meetings.

Or to continue the metaphor, they gather the building materials. This includes bringing *lost* people to Christ and building *found* people together.

The ministry of Priscilla and Aquila was just that—they were initiators in the work of church building.

New church plants need those who will initiate, bring others together, and prepare the soil for a church planter to do his work.

The church planter's job, once he visits a new group, is to help build the members together whereby everyone becomes an initiator, and no one "leads" the group except for the Lord Jesus Christ Himself.

But before that can happen, at least one or two people need to initiate and prepare the site.

Important observation: If the initiators do not take the second step and invite an apostolic worker in to lay the foundation and equip the new church to function under Christ, then those initiators will become the clergy of the group by default. Whether this happens wittingly or unwittingly, it will occur. Everyone in the group will look to these people for direction. The result? The group will become a miniature version of the institutional church.

In my observation, the above scenario is happening all too often in our day.

Church planters, because they are itinerant and constitute an outside resource for the group, are supposed to keep this from occurring.

(Note that I'm speaking of church planters who are safe and trustworthy. False "apostles" abound. Workers who are legalistic, corrupt, arrogant, sectarian, or elitist end up doing great damage to the kingdom of God.)

Preparing the Site and Cultivating the Ground

Let's quickly look at how Priscilla and Aquila prepared the way for Paul to raise up churches.

Before Paul went to the city of Ephesus to plant a church there, he sent Priscilla and Aquila ahead of him to prepare the building site (Acts 18:19). Priscilla and Aquila visited the synagogue to look for open hearts. They then opened their home to gather "building materials" for the new church plant (Acts 18:26). When Paul returned to Ephesus to plant the church (Acts 19), the members met in the home of Priscilla and Aquila (1 Cor. 16:19—Paul wrote this letter from Ephesus).

Later, Priscilla and Aquila went back to their home city (Rome) and opened up their house for a new church to gather (Rom. 16:3–5). As we've already seen, Paul sent the couple back to Rome early to prepare the way for him to visit the city—just as he did in Ephesus (see chapter 1). As the New Testament closes, we find Priscilla and Aquila back in Ephesus (2 Tim. 4:19—Timothy was in Ephesus when Paul wrote to him).

The preparation work of Priscilla and Aquila followed the same pattern of John the Baptist. John "prepared the way" for the first apostle—Jesus Christ—to do His work (Heb. 3:1). It's not without significance that many of the Lord's disciples were first followers of John the Baptist. Consequently, John "prepared the site" and "cultivated the ground" before Jesus raised up the first embryonic expression of the church—which was made up of the twelve disciples and some women in Galilee.

In a similar way, Cornelius, one of the first Gentile converts, gathered the building materials before Peter came, and laid the foundation for the church in Caesarea. The text says,

The following day he [Peter] arrived in Caesarea.
Cornelius was expecting them and had called together
his relatives and close friends. (Acts 10:24)

Jesus' reference to "the person of peace" is also along the same lines (Luke 10:6).

Helps for Gathering Critical Mass

Perhaps the Lord has called you to the site-preparation ministry of Priscilla and Aquila in the city where you live. Or perhaps He desires to send you to another city to prepare the ground for a new church plant there.

Either way, here are some practical suggestions for gathering a group of people together who have a common vision for meeting as an organic church.

1. Pray regularly that the Lord will raise up an organic church in your area. Ask Him to cause you to meet those who are interested in organic church life.

2. If you have the gift of evangelism, seek to bring others to the Lord who will become the ground floor of the new church. Become friends with unbelievers, and share Christ with them as the Spirit of God leads.

3. Begin passing out books to your friends on organic church life. My book *Reimagining Church* was written for this very purpose.

4. Have a barbecue or picnic, and invite those who have read these books to your home to discuss the possibilities of meeting as an organic house church. Do this regularly if need be.

5. If you have friends who aren't readers, pass out the little booklet *The Organic Church* by Milt Rodriguez (www.TheRebuilders. org/organicbook.html).

6. Begin a book group in your local area. Advertise in your local Christian bookstores, newspapers, Christian radio, Barnes & Nobles, Borders, Books-a-Millions, www.MeetUp.com, etc. Meet weekly and discuss one to three chapters at a time. Offer snacks and refreshments. I'd suggest choosing a book that's listed at www.HouseChurchResource.org (see the "Books" link).

7. Visit www.HouseChurchResource.org, and click on the "Find an Organic Church" link. Fill out the form in its entirety.

8. Invite a church planter to host a weekend conference in your city. (If you are interested in exploring this option, fill out the "Invite a Church Planter" form at www.HouseChurchResource.org.)

The rest of this section of the book is designed to give a group of Christians who wish to begin meeting some initial steps in their journey. The content of these chapters is based on my experience of gathering with organic churches for the last twenty-one years. The lessons learned have come out of a great deal of experimentation, profound failure, and not a few serendipitous discoveries granted by God's grace.

The church, when planted in the soil of Christ, is a living organism. Thus church planters are like observing botanists. They learn by watching the life of a church take root, flourish, pass through seasons, ward off life-threatening pests, struggle for its life against dry spells, sprout, and reseed.

I make no pretense that the ideas presented in this section can't be improved upon. They simply embody what I've found to work in giving God's people a beginning. A beginning toward the discovery of the *experience* of the body of Christ. To put it another way, this section is designed to create a womb for the church of Jesus Christ to be born in a given place.

More specifically, the following pages are designed to lay a ground floor for a devoted group of eight or more believers over a six-month (or longer) period.[1]

My strong suggestion is to read this part of the book as a group over the span of four to five weeks. You may do this in one of two ways:

1. When you meet, each of you takes turns reading a page. Read one or two chapters per meeting.

---

1   According to my experience, eight adults who are devoted to developing a common life in Christ constitute critical mass for a long-standing organic church to begin. The text where Jesus said, "When two or three are gathered together in my name," in Matt. 18 is often taken out of context. In that text, the Lord is discussing a church discipline situation where two or three members of a local assembly may represent the Lord's mind when trying to restore an unrepentant member. Matt. 18, therefore, cannot be used to support the idea that two individuals make up a local *ekklesia*.

2. Each week, have everyone read one or two chapters on their own. When you come together, discuss what you have read.

Either way, I suggest you create a concrete plan to implement the content. So bringing a calendar to these meetings would be very wise.

My hope is that the Lord would breathe on these words and make them a catalyst for restoring body life all over this globe.

CHAPTER 14

FIVE UNMOVABLE PRINCIPLES

A great deal more failure is the result of an excess of caution than of bold experimentation with new ideas. The frontiers of the kingdom of God were never advanced by men and women of caution.

—J. Oswald Sanders

If you've read this far, then you are probably embarking on what may turn out to be the greatest spiritual adventure of your life—the discovery of gathering under the headship of Jesus Christ in an organic way.

In this chapter, I would like to introduce you to five unmovable principles. If you can embrace them—and manage to remember them—it will inoculate you from a bundle of problems and disappointments that await you.

Principle 1: Become like little children.

One sure thing that will kill body life is the belief that you—an individual—are more mature, more gifted, and more spiritual than the rest of the group.

Perhaps in your last church you were regarded as a spiritual giant. Perhaps you were even a minister in some capacity. Perhaps you have been outside the institutional church for years and have experienced all kinds of supernatural activity. Perhaps you were in an organic church in the past, so you feel that you're more experienced than the rest of the group.

If so, please keep this in mind. There is one experience you have never had. It's an experience that is totally new to you. *It is the experience of being built together with all of the brothers and sisters who are in your present group.* It's the experience of being in a face-to-face community with Jesus Christ as the group's only Head. This changes the playing field dramatically. And it makes everyone a beginner.

If you wish to discover Jesus Christ corporately in a fresh way, then become like a little child. Drop your agendas. Drop your ambitions. Drop what you think you are in the Lord. Drop what you think your gifts are. And become a humble brother or sister in Christ.

One of the greatest—and most common—tragedies of a new organic church plant is for its members to transfer pounds of institutional baggage from their religious background straight into the new group. When this happens, the church becomes nothing more than a scaled-down, small-is-beautiful version of a particular stripe of the institutional church.[1] Further, if you have people in the group who come from different religious backgrounds, the only chance you have for staying together is if everyone agrees to come in with a clean slate.

That being said, if the Lord will lead your group, you will be unlearning many things. You will be discarding a great deal of excess baggage that weighs you down. This baggage touches the way we pray, the way we sing, the kinds of songs we sing, the vocabulary we use, the way we see ourselves, the way we see the Lord, the way we approach the Bible, the way we share, etc. In short, it makes what should be a light burden heavy.

The most important ingredient for a new organic church is to strip down to Christ alone. Doing so will give the Lord a clear shot at revealing Himself to you in a new way. He will be free to express Himself in a way that is natural, organic, and free of traditional baggage.

So come up to ground zero. Put your gifts, your "ministry," and your ambitions at the foot of the cross. And let God, in His time, raise up whatever He wishes to raise up.

I assure you whatever comes up out of the ground will look quite different from what it did in the past. This is the principle of resurrection: It is only by death that new life is produced. And what dies comes back in a different form.

If you are not prepared to do this, you will severely hamstring the life of the church. I implore you, therefore, to come with a heart

---

1   By "institutional baggage," I am referring to those unhealthy and unscriptural practices and concepts that we have unwittingly picked up in our previous institutional church experiences. (Note that not everything that the institutional church does is unhealthy or unscriptural. I owe my salvation and my baptism to the institutional church.)

to discover the Lord all over again with the brothers and sisters with whom you will be churching. For it is to such—those who have become like little children—that the kingdom of God is given.

You are stepping into a world where most of you have never been. You will be taking responsibility for your meetings and for the affairs of the church. Not as an individual, but as a people.

For this reason, it's important that there is no one acting in the capacity of a clergyman in your group. Participation will come from each of you as you learn to function as members of Christ's body. Leadership will come from the Holy Spirit through the body. Sometimes it will come from the weakest. Other times it will come from the strongest. Decisions will be hammered out by consensus. Specialized gifts and functions will emerge naturally in time.

Burn this into the circuitry of your brain: Everyone in the group should be on equal footing. There should not be a local member of the group who is designated as the leader or facilitator. Forfeit this and the book you are reading at this moment will be of little value to you.[2]

Principle 2: Your feelings will get hurt.

Institutional religion has a way of hiding our flaws. It also has a way of safeguarding and insulating us from each other. In an organic church, we get to know one another very well. That means that what we are in the natural gets exposed. Authentic church life is a house of mirrors.

---

2   The exception to this principle is if you have a church planter who is equipping the group. If that is the case, he should be working himself out of a job. He should not meet with you all the time, and he should have *real* plans of leaving the group on its own after he lays the foundation.

One of the most profound things that you will learn in a face-to-face community is the utter depths that the fall has marked on your soul. Consequently, it's inevitable that you will hurt one another. This is one of the cardinal laws that I have discovered in twenty-one years of living in body life. John Ortberg wrote a book titled *Everybody's Normal Till You Get to Know Them.* That title sums up body life pretty well.

Add to this principle the following sentence: *You will not get your own way in the church.* So learn to surrender. Discover the spiritual secret of relinquishing control and forfeiting your way. There is something called a cross. And it's found at full force in body life. The cross means death to self. It means loss. It means suffering. You will meet the cross in one another. It is inevitable.

Body life is a holy wedding of glory and gore—agony and ecstasy. This journey will be the most difficult adventure in your life. But it may very well be the most glorious.

The principle of the cross is designed to transform you. It's designed to bring life to your brothers and sisters in Christ. If you get your own way all the time, then the Lord is not getting His way. If you are forfeiting your way, then you are allowing the Lord Jesus to build His own house—and your labor will not be in vain.

If you can accept that the cross is embedded in the DNA of church life, it will spare you from having unrealistic expectations. Keep this in mind. When someone hurts your feelings, at that moment, your spiritual mettle is being fiercely tested. Your reaction will reveal volumes about yourself. But this is God's wonderful design of transforming you into His glorious image.

To frame it another way, you will never learn the virtues of forbearance, patience, endurance, long-suffering, extending mercy and forgiveness until you are thrown together with a group of very imperfect people who are putting absolute strains on your Christian character.

I offer you an image: The members of an organic church are living stones that are being welded together to form a dwelling place for the Lord. In order for those stones to be built together, they require a great deal of cutting, chiseling, sanding, and refining. If you can remember that these deeper virtues are being worked out when you face difficulties in the group, it will carry you a long way during the painful periods. The secret: Allow the Lord to thicken your skin, and you will survive body life.

Principle 3: Be patient with the progress of the group.

Meeting in a home doesn't constitute the birth of church life. A church, in its purest form, takes time to be born. It took approximately nine months for you to be born. In that time, your mother experienced growth pains, sickness, uncomfortable positions, and major adjustments to her wardrobe and to her eating and sleeping patterns.

It's similar with the birth of an *ekklesia*. The church is a living organism. Therefore, it takes time to be born. Starting something is human; but birth is divine. Birthing a church is territory staked out exclusively by divinity. It is not a human proposition.

I entreat you, therefore, to be patient. You will be learning to use instincts you have never before used. More important, you are beginning a journey to discover your Lord like never before. Not as an individual, but as a people.

Before the foundation of a new house can be laid, the lot must be thoroughly cleared. Trees, brush, and debris all must be removed. Your first six months (plus) are the "clearing phase" of your life as a new church. The exercises in this book are designed to give your group a clean slate upon which to lay a rock-solid foundation.

During this clearing phase, a great deal of unlearning will occur. A great deal of deprogramming and detoxification. A great deal of tearing down of the old mind-sets, the old mentality, the old vocabulary, and the old practices. A discarding of the methods of operation that you picked up by being part of institutional Christianity. In place of that, there will grow up among you a new mind-set, a new mentality, a new way of operating, a new vocabulary, and a new way to know the Lord and express Him together.

This all takes time. Lots of time.

Laying hold of authentic body life is the 100-mile walk rather than the 40-yard dash.

Therefore, body life demands infinite patience. You may think at times that it can't possibly work. That it's hopeless. That the die has been miscast, and you were handed the wrong bundle of people to church with. You may feel at times that the group simply refuses to do what you want them to do, the church will not grow fast enough for you, etc.

Impatience with the birth of church life is a monumental hurdle that those who subscribe to a microwave-on-high-for-two-minutes philosophy will have to face squarely. Task-oriented, program-driven people will have a run-in with the slow pace of body life. But no one can hurry the birthing process. That is God's business.

Let me remind you that you are moving away from a religious service on Sunday morning where you mostly sit and listen—toward an organic gathering of new creations, discovering afresh how to express Jesus Christ corporately. That's no small shift. It's as large as the universe.

So I exhort you to stick with it, regardless of how slow the pace. If you can manage to endure, you will discover a Lord who is all-sufficient. But remember—He moves according to His own clock. And His clock almost always ticks slower than ours.

Principle 4: People will leave your group.

This should be chiseled in marble. Let's face it. In the minds of most Christians, it's flat-out strange to go against the conventional current of having a paid pastor, an in-place Sunday school program, a church building, and a church service that's centered on a worship team and a forty-five-minute sermon.

If you live in the Western world, you have options. Countless options. You are accustomed to choosing from a raft of different automobiles, ice-cream flavors, and brands of cologne. In the city where you live, there are most likely hundreds of churches, Bible studies, and parachurch organizations that you may join.

The situation was drastically different in the first century. There was only one option if you were a Christian. If you came to Christ, you became part of the one and only church in your city. And that church met in homes without a clergy. In the New Testament era, coming to Christ was the equivalent of being membered to His body.

What does this mean for you? It simply means that the only way you will manage to hang together for the long haul is if you have come to the place where you have run out of options.

Meeting in a home without a modern pastor has a pretty hefty price tag attached to it. The meetings are now in *your* hands. What to do with the children is now a problem that *you* as a group must resolve. Difficulties with the other members is a challenge that *you* must tackle. Add to that, authentic church life will not work if you come to the meetings only to receive and not to give. And giving requires spiritual preparation. It requires time. It requires energy.

So get clear at the outset that there's an excellent chance that some of the people who are reading this book with you will not be around a few months from now. Let alone a few weeks. And there are endless reasons why they will leave.

But here is the most important thing I wish to say to you. When people leave, I beg you not to pressure or persuade them to stay. And more important, do not speak ill of them when they go. On top of that, it's of utmost importance that you refrain from imputing evil motives to their hearts. I have watched the profound destruction that judging motives does to relationships. The damage is devastating, and it has a ripple effect that injures others.

The Lord Jesus condemned this practice, saying, "Judge not lest you be judged. For you will be judged by the same standard that you have judged others." These are thundering words. The Lord gave peculiar insight into what happens when a person judges the motives of another. The one who finds fault with his brother and detects a speck of wood in his eye is exposing the fact that he is guilty of having a cedar tree in his own. The speck is actually a small chip off the cedar tree.

Consequently, when someone judges the heart motives of another, they are in effect projecting what is in their own heart onto another person. Simply put, to impute ill motives onto another human being is to expose what is in our own hearts. Only Jesus Christ has the right and the ability to see into the motives of someone's heart. We have no such capacity.

I implore you, therefore, to take the high road when people leave your group. Accept what they say at face value instead of second-guessing their intentions. In fact, if you really wish to hit a high watermark, bless and speak well of them when they leave. Especially *after* they leave.

To do so incarnates a monumental breakthrough in the kingdom of God. It also speaks volumes about your group. Namely, that your church is not built on fear, elitism, sectarianism, or religious obligation—but on freedom. And an atmosphere of liberty and freedom is an evidence of the presence of God's Spirit. Note that freedom includes the freedom to leave without negative consequences.

Principle 5: People will experience exciting spiritual growth and healing.

Even though organic church is difficult, it provides a context in which God's people can experience significant spiritual growth, maturity, and healing. This is because the organic expression of the church is our natural habitat. It's the God-ordained environment that believers are called to live out their lives. It is the native nurturing ground for the Christian. The mutual participation, encouragement, and loving atmosphere that organic churches provide cause believers to make significant strides in their spiritual walk. Discipleship (as it's often called today) was never meant to take place outside of this context.

Time and again people have testified that experiencing open-participatory meetings and authentic community has accelerated their spiritual maturity, love, devotion, following of the Lord, and the expression of their gifts. Therefore, the combination of knowing the cross of Christ in close-knit community and learning to live by God's life rather than our own creates transformation.

I've never seen these five principles change. If you can manage to keep them in mind, they will increase your chances for survival dramatically. Write them down. Revisit them. And remind one another of them from time to time. Let us now turn our attention to your corporate meetings.

CHAPTER 15

LEARNING HOW TO MEET

An ounce of experience is worth a ton of theory.

—Benjamin Franklin

I make no claim that what you will read in the following pages is the only way to begin. It is, however, the *best way* that I have seen so far.

Before we delve into this subject, I want to say a few words about the language we have been conditioned to use. There are two phrases that will not serve you well as you move forward: "church service" (or simply "the service") and "going to church."

Now that you are learning how to meet under the headship of Jesus Christ in simplicity, you are forever finished with "church services." Services belong to institutions. They are ritualistic, performance-based ceremonies. The early Christians never had "services." Instead, they had "meetings." This is the word that is employed throughout the New Testament when the early Christians assembled together to worship and display Christ.

Second, you are no longer "going to church." The church, or *ekklesia*, is the body of Christ, which assembles together. It's not a place to go. It's not an edifice. To call a church a building is like calling your mother a skyscraper. You are going to "a meeting," and you are part of the church.

It will take some time for you to evacuate these unbiblical concepts from your thinking and adjust your vocabulary. What we say reveals a great deal about what we believe.

Let us now move on to the practical arrangements of your meetings. Some of these practical suggestions will be obvious to some of you. But rest assured, my experience has it that they are not obvious to everyone. Hence the details.

Practical Arrangements

1. Find a home in which to meet. Hopefully, the person who has the largest living room will be willing to host the meetings. (Note: Meeting places can range from homes to garages, to office rooms, to clubhouses, etc.)

If the person who is hosting the meeting lives fifty miles away from everyone, that won't work. It's important to find a home that is central to where most of the group lives. Make certain that the person (or couple) who hosts the meetings understands that they do not own the church.

Those who are hosting the meetings have the prerogative to lay down the house rules (i.e., whether or not to take your shoes off, to park in a certain spot, etc.). And it is important that the group respects those rules. If you have several people who are willing to host the meetings, you may want to rotate homes.

2. Decide when you will have your meetings. I suggest that you have your corporate meetings weekly—either on a Saturday evening, a Sunday morning, or a Sunday afternoon. Two principles should guide your decision: consensus and edification. Consensus: Everyone participates in the decision. Edification: Decide on a day when everyone is most often available to meet for at least four hours. Child care may be a determining factor as well. We will come back to that later. (Note: You may wish to revisit and negotiate the time and day of your meetings as the group gets larger.)

3. Be conscious of temperature. If you are not meeting in the winter, be sure to turn your air conditioner down to at least 69 degrees half an hour before everyone arrives. The reason is that once the group shows up and begins singing, the room will heat up faster than you can blink.

I'll add to this something that's all too often overlooked. When the room gets stuffy, a window or two should be cracked for ventilation. Awareness to temperature is often sorely neglected in church life. It needs constant reminding.

The church is now in your hands. Therefore, great care must be given to it. If something breaks (like a thermostat or an air conditioner), take responsibility to fix it. Your survival depends upon giving care and attention to such practical matters.

4. Make a noble effort to be punctual to the meetings. This is vital. It also represents one of the greatest hurdles that you will face as a new church. One that you cannot afford to be slack on. If you start dribbling into the meeting five minutes late, it will continue to escalate until your meetings will not begin until thirty minutes later. The net effect? *People will stop coming to your meetings.*

Institutional churches can get away with persistent latecomers. But not so with you. Open-participatory meetings require everyone to be on time. Your survival depends on it. If this begins to slip, someone should make the group aware that people are coming in late.

Here are three tips that I have learned over the years that will help people to be punctual:

(1) If the meeting begins at 10:30 a.m., encourage everyone to arrive at 10:15 a.m.

(2) When there are four people present at the meeting time, those four people should not wait for the others to trickle in. Instead, those four should begin the meeting. If the meetings always start on time, even among a few, it will provoke the others to be on time. But if the group waits until everyone shows up, people will get the unmistakable impression that it's acceptable to be late. The problem will persist until you find your group dead in the water.

(3) If all else fails, have a lockout. Lock the doors at the appointed starting time. That should solve your problem. (I'm just kidding.)

5. *When you meet, be sure to announce the time and place of your next meeting before everyone leaves.* I have observed that if such an announcement is not made, many will not show up for the next meeting. The best time to make this announcement is at the end of the meeting.

6. *Be sure to maintain your bathroom before every meeting.* This may seem silly, but I have known people who visited a church that gathers in a home never to return again for one reason: the condition

of the bathroom. The three key things to remember about bathrooms are as follows:

(1) Be sure that there is an adequate amount of toilet paper available.

(2) Be sure that there is a towel, soap, and a plunger accessible. (Yes, a plunger.)

(3) Be sure that there is a way to lock the bathroom door from the inside. In addition, it would not hurt to make sure the bathroom is clean before every meeting.

7. *The group should take great care to clean up after every meeting.* If a person is hosting the meetings in their home, the burden of cleanup should not fall upon their shoulders. Instead, the rest of the group should carry the cleanup burden—including the men. Depending on the size of the group, everyone should participate in cleanup or two different people (preferably brothers) should bear the responsibility each month. This would include taking down the chairs, vacuuming the rug, sweeping the floor, cleaning up the kitchen, etc.

8. *Arrange the chairs in a way that promotes open sharing.* There is a way of arranging chairs that came out of Plymouth, England, in the nineteenth century. To my mind, it's better than setting up chairs in rows or in a circle. The reason is that it invites face-to-face communication and brings everyone as close as possible. I suggest putting the chairs (including comfy couches and sofas) in the form of a small square. As numbers increase, form a larger square of chairs around the smaller square (see diagram below). Those who enjoy sitting on the floor can conveniently sit in the middle of the square on top of pillows and/or blankets.

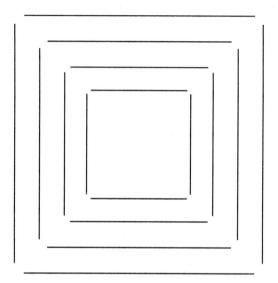

9. If the meeting is crowded, be sure that the paths to and from the front door and the bathroom are clear. Do your best on this. It's easy to forget. It is incredibly distracting when people are trying to climb over a mound of breathing bodies just to get to the bathroom or enter the home.

10. Give visitors an opportunity to introduce themselves. If you have visitors, someone in the group should ask them to share who they are, where they are from, and what brought them to your gathering. The best time to do this is after you sing or at the end of your meeting. Another oft-neglected practice of many churches is to follow up with your visitors. Have someone greet them at the end of the meeting. Get their contact information. Give them a call during the week. Ask them how they liked the meeting. And invite them back. It is essential that you make visitors feel not only welcome, but also wanted. If not, you are headed toward devolving into an us-four-and-no-more clique. Churches that suffer from that disease end up losing more members than they gain.

11. Come to the meetings informally dressed. Men, please do not dress up in your Sunday best. Women, kindly leave the fancy-shmancy clothes at home. Dress modestly, but informally. You are through with ritualistic services where you watch, listen, and minimally take part. You are through with spectator church. You are learning how to participate in an informal gathering of God's people.[1]

12. Please turn off your cell phones or set them to vibrate. This is common courtesy. I've been in many a meeting where someone was trying to share, and the cold chill of someone's cell-phone ringer halted the entire meeting.

Meeting Content

I suggest that the content of your meetings for at least the first six months contain four elements.

1. SING TOGETHER.

Learn to sing as a corporate group of believers. Learn to sing as the body of Christ without a song leader or music director. On top of that, learn new songs. Many new songs.

My suggestion is that for the first year, don't introduce any musical instruments. Instead, learn to sing together a cappella. Why? Because for centuries we Christians have been conditioned to let instruments control our singing. We sit and we wait for a guitar (or piano) to tell us when to begin singing and when to stop. A song leader will actually kill corporate singing. You will be stuck back under a music minister. Therefore, I urge you to lay down all instruments for the first year and learn to sing corporately.

---

1   Dressing up for church is a fairly recent invention. See chapter 6 of *Pagan Christianity* for details.

By removing instruments and singing a cappella, you are winning back singing into the hands of all of God's people. Once the church owns her own singing where there is no song leader present, then musical instruments may be introduced without inhibiting body functioning. However, those playing instruments should learn to *follow* the singing rather than *lead* it.

A note to musicians: Consider the possibility that the Lord would desire for you to lay down your talent at His cross so that His people could rise to their calling of singing corporately. Unfortunately, I've met some musicians who were not willing to pay that price. I hope to God that there would be more gifted people who preferred the functioning of the Lord's body over their individual gifts.

In the next chapter, I will address this subject more thoroughly. We will discuss how to write and rewrite songs and how to build your own church songbook. The goal is that you will learn to sing as the body of Christ without any props or song leaders. In the church after God's heart, every member is a song leader. You may think that this is utterly impossible. But let me assure you that it is not only possible, but it's also a discovery that once experienced, you will never want to forfeit.

2. SHARE TOGETHER.

What follows are five exercises that I suggest you try for at least the first six months plus. (How long you do them will largely depend on the size of your group.)

The Weeks to Follow: Exercise 1

Each week, one of you tells your life story. This will include your testimony of how you came to Christ and the story of your Christian life up until the present day. Your life story will also include what brought you to assemble with the present group of believers.

Be creative if you like. Include songs, poems, photographs, photo slides, video clips—anything you wish that will help you communicate your story. Each of you will have the entire meeting to tell everyone your life story in whatever way you wish.

If someone is not comfortable sharing their story, they are under no obligation to do so. (I've yet to meet someone who wasn't. But they no doubt exist.) Also, at this stage, it's not wise to tell gruesome details about extremely personal matters from your past. This will make many in your group feel very uncomfortable. So please use discernment about how personal you get.

Do this every week until everyone has told their life stories.

Note that there are some people who can tell their story in five minutes or less. In such cases, it falls upon the group to ask this person questions and draw the story out of them. As new people are added to the group, give them an opportunity to tell their life stories also. Everyone should get an entire meeting to do this. When everyone has finished, go on to exercise 2.

The Weeks to Follow: Exercise 2

As we have already seen, the preached Word of God has incredible community-forming properties that cannot be explained rationally. Receiving Christ-centered ministry, therefore, is important for a young church plant.

If you go to www.HouseChurchResource.org, you will find a list of foundational, Christ-centered messages given by various Christian workers. Select one of the mp3s or Audio CD sets that are available on the site.

Each time you come together, listen to one CD or mp3 from the set. The most important part: When the message is finished, share with one another what you received from it. Do not focus on anything negative. Instead, share what ministered to you, what touched you, what stirred you, what new insight you discovered or saw about the Lord and His church.

A number of new churches have done this exercise, and it has profited them greatly. It's the next best thing to being at a live event where a spiritual foundation of Jesus Christ is being laid. Consider giving this a try, and you may also find it to be of great help. When you have finished listening to the messages together, begin exercise 3.

The Weeks to Follow: Exercise 3

Each week, two people will bring to the meeting one song that has special value to them. The song can be performed or written by a Christian or a non-Christian artist. Each person will share how he or she saw the Lord through the song they bring.

They will either play the song on tape or CD, or sing/perform it for the rest of the group. Or both. They will then take as much time as they need to share how the lyrics and/or the music have special value to them. Namely, how does the song minister the Lord to them? The sharing will be open for group participation and interaction. Everyone in the group is encouraged to comment in an edifying way on each person's song and what they saw through it. When everyone has done this, go on to exercise 4.

The Weeks to Follow: Exercise 4

Each week, two people will bring to the meeting two of their favorite passages from the Bible. Each person will read the passage to the group and explain what they understand the passage to mean. They will then encourage the group with why it has special meaning for them. The sharing will be open for group participation and interaction. Attention, men: Please stay away from theological discourses, debate, and heady, arcane expoundings of the text. Your sharing should be personal and from the heart. When everyone has done this, go on to exercise 5.

The Weeks to Follow: Exercise 5

Each week, two people will share what they would like their life to look like in five years. This will include their ambitions and aspirations, relating to both earthly and spiritual matters. Cover the waterfront on this. Let the group hear your hopes, aspirations, and dreams. The group is encouraged to interact and comment on what's shared.

A word of caution: Guard strongly against the tendency to throw rocks at the institutional church when you gather. If you have bitterness or anger against the religious system, I implore you to bring it to the Lord and leave it with Him. If you need to vent, find one or two people whom you trust. Meet with them outside the church meeting and vent all you want about your hurts. *Then let it die.* A group that licks its wounds and reacts against the traditional church will eventually destroy itself. Your reason for meeting is positive. It is unto and for Jesus Christ. It's not reactionary or negative.

3. EAT TOGETHER.

This is a pillar upon which true body life is built. Have a potluck meal either before or after your sharing time. If you eat first, some people may have difficulty keeping their eyes open during the sharing. (Food has a way of causing people to descend from alertness to a mild coma.) On the other hand, eating before the sharing time allows everyone to interact socially as soon as the meeting begins. It also can solve the punctuality problem if you happen to have one.

There are three main ways to organize a potluck. (If you discover a fourth, great.)

1. Someone in the group tells each person what to bring (e.g., "Sandy, can you bring two boxes of fried chicken? Tommy, can you bring two liters of Diet Pepsi? Jimmy, would you mind bringing some green vegetables?" etc.)

2. In a previous meeting, pass a sheet around the room that has the major food groups listed. Everyone fills in what they will bring.

3. Everyone blindly brings something, and you hope to God that there is enough food as well as a healthy balance of each food group.

(A note about the poor: If you have people in your group who are desperately poor and can't contribute by bringing food, here's a suggestion. Ask them to come over to one of the believer's homes and help cook some of the meal. Encourage them to contribute in some way instead of continually coming empty-handed.)

If you end up eating before the meeting, make sure that someone alerts everyone when the eating is over. Move to the meeting room, and begin your sharing.

Eating is a family activity. It helps to build solidarity among family members. People feel much freer and less inhibited to share their lives and thoughts over a meal. There is a mysterious element in a meal that binds people together in an uncommon way. For this reason, the early Christians ate together frequently. And they understood themselves to be the household or family of God.

Spend the better part of a whole day meeting and then eating. Joke a lot. Laugh a lot. Good, wholesome humor and fun is a wonderful thing. This helps everyone in the group to feel relaxed and openly share about themselves.

4. HAVE FUN TOGETHER.

Making "play" a part of your church life is an indispensable ingredient for the group's success. One of the most important things you are learning during this season is how not to be religious. You are discovering how to be "real" and how to cultivate a feeling of safety with one another. You are also learning to unpack years of traditional baggage. *You are detoxing.*

We have all been conditioned to be religious creatures. Consequently, whenever Christians meet together in a spiritual setting, it's exceedingly difficult for them to be normal. Instead, we turn religious. We hide behind a pretentious mask. Our vocabulary, our style of speaking, and our praying all change when we get together with others for a "Christian" meeting.

It's this sort of religious spirit that will destroy a group of people. Let me put it this way. Suppose that there are twelve of you who are meeting. If you stay religious, you will divide into more fragments than a dried-out piece of cornbread.

The early church was born in an atmosphere of spiritual authenticity. The body of Christ breathes the air of informality. It's void of ritualism, legalism, professionalism, and religiosity.

By learning to get to know one another in an informal, nonreligious atmosphere, you are providing a womb for authentic body life to be born. Religiosity is not spirituality. The former will bring death to a group of Christians.

So eat, sing, share your life stories, and have fun. Keep believing that the Lord is going to make your walk together beautiful.

If the truth be told: The biggest task that you have over the next year is to learn to get to know one another *really* well. And to learn to get along outside of a religious context. Simply getting to know one another and getting along is a task as big as the ocean. But if you can pull it off, it will give you the right ground upon which to build a rock-solid foundation.

In my observation, the reason why there are so many splits among God's people is because we Christians really don't know one another well, nor do we trust one another. In addition, the members of your group will never be fully released to share in an open meeting if they do not feel safe, accepted, and known by the other members. They will persistently hold their cards very close to their vest.

Common Questions

WHAT DO WE DO WITH THE CHILDREN?

I think this question should be reframed to "What do we do *for* the children?" This is the singularly most asked question in the world of organic churching. Take heed: I have seen churches crash and burn before they ever got off the ramp because they could not agree on this issue!

Before I give my suggestions, I would like to state a few principles that go straight to the heart of our problems on this score. First, in the West, adults tend to neglect their children, abuse them, or worship them. Christians included.

Second, it's all too possible to sacrifice one's family on the altar of the church (1 Tim. 5:8). But it's equally possible to sacrifice the church of Jesus Christ on the altar of the family (Matt. 10:34–38; 12:47–50; Mark 10:29–30; Luke 14:26).

That said, you will all do yourselves a huge favor if you can agree to go along with some variation or combination of the following suggestions for a year. After which time, if some in the group wish to try something different, support them in doing so. I would only ask that you be honest with yourselves if the "something different" is not working.

Children are in virtually every organic church. And the question of what to do with and for them during the meetings will remain a quandary as long as the earth exists. After twenty-one years of experimenting with scores of different ways to resolve the matter, I have made the following observations:

1. When small children are in a meeting where adults are trying to worship the Lord and share deep spiritual things, the children are miserable because they are bored and do not understand what's being said.

2. The adults are miserable because the children are distracting them. It makes it incredibly difficult for them to worship, concentrate, and share.

3. Children are much happier when they are having fun.

4. Children view "church" in a positive light only when they can associate fun with it. (God created children to enjoy fun and play.)

5. Children learn a great deal about the Lord by watching their parents interact with the other members of the body in day-to-day community life.

6. The primary responsibility for a child's moral training and spiritual education does not fall upon the church. It falls upon the parents.

7. If children are old enough to understand what goes on in a church meeting, and they have a genuine desire to attend, they should be encouraged to do so.

On the heels of these observations, here is what I would suggest. Virtually all of the churches I have gathered with or worked with over the last two decades have found these suggestions to be the best solutions available:

🌱 Hire a competent teenager to oversee the children while they play together during the singing and the sharing time. If you cannot find child care on a given day or you do not wish to take this option, have some in the group rotate watching the children each week. (The disadvantage is that they will have to miss some of the church meetings.) Include the children during the meals. Children will look forward to the opportunity of playing with their peers when the church meets. It will constitute "fun" for them.

❧ If the home in which you meet is too small to have the children in another room wherein they will not distract the meeting, have them play together at a nearby house.

❧ If you have to bring an infant into the meeting, please walk out if the infant begins to cry. That way the others will not be distracted.

❧ Every two to four months, have a special meeting just for the children. Give an entire meeting over to them. Prepare skits, songs, games, comedy routines, and other activities for them. Have a comedy talent night where the adults entertain the children. You may even want to plan a special "mystery" or "adventure" trip for them. Or even a scavenger hunt. Or a tea party for the girls. If you have enough children, hold a softball game or a

water-balloon fight between the adults and
the kids. Have a special slumber party for the
women and the girls. Have a camping trip
for the men and the boys. The things you
can do for the little ones are as limitless as
your creativity. These special meetings will be
unforgettable for the children. And they will
be unforgettable for you as well.

✤ If someone feels burdened to teach the little
children Bible lessons, they should feel free
to open their home on another day to have a
special children's meeting. This can be done
weekly, bimonthly, or monthly. The meeting
can include children's songs, etc. Each parent
is free to decide whether or not they wish to
include their children in this. No one should
feel pressured one way or the other.

Related note: Please don't make the profound mistake of trying
to cram "everything" into one meeting during the week (e.g.,
sharing, worship, learning songs, fellowship, sharing needs, hashing
out problems, ministering to the children, etc.). *This simply will not
work.* Church life is family life. It takes the whole of your life, not a
small slice of it. You are learning to develop a communal life together
with other believers. The church, therefore, is not a one-day-a-week
adventure. If the latter is your outlook—and you "just don't have the
time" for the group—then gathering outside the institutional church

is simply not for you. You would be much happier in the low-volume, low-commitment, once-a-week services that the institutional church offers.

WHAT ABOUT BIBLE STUDY?

The concept of "Bible study" is fairly new. Its origins date back to nineteenth-century America. My observation is that if you begin your church-life experience with Bible study as it's traditionally practiced, the group will splinter rather quickly. If not, it will probably produce a single leader (*sola pastora*), and authentic body life will be smothered. The group will turn into a trimmed-down version of the institutional church with a clergy present.

Many contemporary house churches are glamorized Bible studies. They are not the free-flowing, life-giving, open-participatory meetings that are envisioned in the New Testament—which are far richer and less confined than what can often be a heady analysis.

In my experience, it's important to introduce the corporate use of Scripture after you have gotten to know one another very well and detoxified yourselves significantly from religiosity.[2] When the Scriptures are introduced, they should be introduced as a *means* to fellowship with the Lord, plumb His depths, and discover His riches. Not as a tool to swell one another's craniums with increased academic knowledge. The former will be edifying to the group; the latter will eventually fracture it.

---

2   Keep in mind that the primary audience of this book is Christians who have spent some time in the institutional church. I have friends who plant nontraditional churches chiefly among unbelievers and very new Christians. The dynamics of such groups are quite different so some of my suggestions may not apply to them.

WHAT ABOUT PRAYER MEETINGS?

For most of my Christian life, I have observed that many Christians have picked up a great deal of artificiality in the way they pray and talk about spiritual matters. This is largely due to imitating bad models. To be more pointed: The way that many Christians pray is abysmal.

In addition, there's a great need among modern believers to find novel ways to connect with the Lord both individually and corporately that go beyond the worn-out tools of petition-prayer and traditional Bible study.

Again, the main need of the group for at least the first six months is to learn to get to know one another outside the context of religious duty. By doing so, you will encounter freedom and reality as well as cultivate an environment of safety. These are the necessary foundations for anything spiritually meaningful to take place. That includes prayer … real, authentic, unpretentious and unreligious, Spirit-inspired prayer. Such prayer will emerge naturally in due season.

Accordingly, my suggestion would be to focus on getting to know each other informally. I would encourage you to let prayer come slowly. If someone wishes to pray, let it come naturally rather than out of religious duty or obligation.

In addition, I would advise against having meetings where everyone offers a prayer request. Why? Two reasons. First, those meetings will no doubt turn out to be highly religious. (In every "prayer-request" meeting I've ever been in, the kinds of things that some Christians ask God to do for them range from the ludicrous to the insane.) Second, those meetings will be the first step down a slippery slope that will eventually become the death knell for your group. That is, meeting in order to get your personal needs met. Such a mind-set will eventually suffocate body life.

Repeat: Let prayer come slowly, naturally, and spontaneously. And when it does come, let it be centered on giving gratitude and praise to the Lord.

Do not condemn yourselves if you have a meeting where there is no prayer. There's a great deal of unlearning and relearning that we Christians need when it comes to communing with the Lord. If the truth be told, most Christians would do well to allow their way of praying to go into death. Only then can the Lord raise up a higher (and more genuine) way to speak to and fellowship with Him.

To quote my friend Robert Banks, the spiritual elements of the church "have their full effect only when they spring from soil that has been well prepared through group members getting to know one another, bonding together, and opening up to God's freedom and flexibility."

WHAT ABOUT EVANGELISM AND REACHING THE LOST?

The time will come when the group will enter into a season of outreach (see chapter 20). However, in this season of beginnings, it's important that a strong foundation first be laid. This is essential for the long-term survival of your church. It will also create a solid and stable refuge for the lost to inhabit.

The foundation of a church is extremely important. And foundations take time to be laid. If a church is well nurtured in the beginning and exposed to the Lord's heart in all things—including

His heart for the lost—outreach will be both natural and organic. It will be free of guilt, duty, and religious obligation. Instead, it will be born in freedom and guided by the Spirit of God Himself in its proper season.

Robert Banks uses the analogy that the beginning phase of church life is like a married couple who has chosen not to have children immediately after the wedding. Instead, they have chosen to give time to form a strong marital bond before they bring others into the family circle. I believe this is great wisdom.

At the same time, if you know unbelievers who are spiritually inclined, feel free to bring them to your meetings. If they like the meetings, encourage them to continue to come. They just might find the Lord in your midst as they behold how real—and nonreligious—you are as Christians.

WHAT ABOUT MEETING ACCORDING TO 1 CORINTHIANS 14:26?

The lessons laid out in this chapter are the groundwork that you will need for having open-participatory, Christ-centered meetings. They are your "training wheels," if you please.

If you've been a Christian in the institutional church, you have been conditioned to be a passive spectator. Your spiritual instincts have essentially gone dormant. The lessons in this book are designed to awaken those instincts and free you from the bondage of being a spectator. But this takes time.

Consequently, if you try to have 1 Corinthians 14:26 meetings without first laying a foundation of getting to know each other in a nonreligious context, your meetings will be fairly colorless. Some people will dominate the entire meeting. Others, who are more timid, will revert back into a pew potato and watch and listen the entire time. In addition, the content will most likely be quite shallow if not contentious.

Having church meetings where everyone functions and reveals Christ deeply in the meetings requires both time and equipping. Most of that equipping will come from the Christ-centered ministry of outside workers who are invited to help the group. The task of Christian workers is to equip God's people to express and reveal the Lord Jesus Christ in His depths through open-participatory meetings and face-to-face community as well as through corporate witness to the lost. This equipping includes fresh approaches to interacting with Scripture, prayer, and corporate sharing.

WHAT DO WE DO ABOUT MONEY AND GIVING?

For at least the first six months, I recommend that every person in the group set aside (on their own) an allotted amount of money every month. This money will be earmarked for the church. It will cover such needs as child care, chairs, songbooks, etc. It would be wise to have extralocal help in the future. So earmark some money to help cover the traveling expenses of those you will invite in to encourage you.

WHAT DO WE DO ABOUT PEOPLE WHO VISIT US BUT WHO DO NOT UNDERSTAND WHAT WE ARE DOING?

Undoubtedly, you are going to have people visit your group who will ask why you aren't having Bible study, why you aren't engaging in street witnessing and passing out gospel tracts, and why you aren't praying for the missionaries in Ouagadougou. And of course, why you're having so much fun together.

If I were part of the group, I would probably tell them that we are turning a new page in our Christian lives where we want things to be organic—out of the soil—rather than mechanical, forced, or driven by human imitation, program, obligation, duty, or guilt. I would also shamelessly admit that we are detoxing from an institutional mind-set and all that goes with it.

If your visitor seems genuinely open and interested, I might even hand them this book. If a visitor has the same longing for the body of Christ that burns within you, they have run out of options, and they have no agenda to push, they will probably hold their nose and take the plunge along with you. (Those who have a personal agenda will either try to push it on the group or never return for another visit.)

SHOULD WE CREATE A CONSTITUTION, BYLAWS, A COVENANT, OR A DOCTRINAL STATEMENT?

I'm inclined to advise against such human props. If you go down the road of defining your fellowship by doctrines or laws or covenants, you will invariably create another sect on top of the thirty-three thousand that already exist. You will also shut out some of God's people before they even get to know you. To quote Jon Zens, "The thicker the constitution, the sooner the group will split." To my mind, these are man-made attempts to control the group or to create commitment within it. If you make the Lord Jesus Christ your focus, the rest will take care of itself.

Practical Exercises

- ❧ Discuss where you will have your corporate meetings.

- ❧ Discuss the time when your meetings will begin.

- ❧ Discuss how you will handle child care.

- ❧ Discuss how you will handle your potlucks.

- ❧ Decide how you are going to handle cleanup after the meetings.

- ❧ Use your calendar to plan out the next month or two of corporate meetings, and discuss what you will do in those meetings (e.g., listening to spoken ministry, selecting who will share their life story on which dates, etc.).

CHAPTER 16

CORPORATE SINGING

Sing to the LORD a new song.

—Psalm 98:1

In this chapter, I want to spread the canvas very wide. My aim is to begin the process of equipping you as a group of believers to function under the headship of Christ. In my experience, functioning begins with singing.

Renewing Our Vocabulary

In many institutional churches, the segment of time when the congregation sings is called "praise and worship." I believe this is misleading and inaccurate.

Praise means to honor, to extol, or to exalt. You can praise the Lord without music and without singing. Worship means to pay homage to. The Hebrew word translated "worship" means to kiss the hand of another. According to Romans 12:2, worship is the church's reasonable service. Worship is a lifestyle of responding to the Lord and loving Him. You can worship God with or without singing and music. Consequently, "praise and worship" should not be employed to refer to your singing time. We praise and worship the Lord all throughout the gathering, not just in the singing.

As a new creature in Christ, singing is part of your species. A Christian who doesn't sing is like a human who doesn't breathe. It's part of our nature as new creatures in Christ to sing. God put melody in the heavens. He also put melody in humanity. Singing is innate to us believers.

The Role of Singing in the Institutional Church

The modern-day practice of music and singing in the institutional church is largely clerical. This has only been dispensed with on a very small scale. In my book *Pagan Christianity*, I dedicate an entire chapter to tracing the origins of the choir director, the music minister, and the worship team in the traditional church. It may be a good idea to read that chapter so that you will get a handle on the vast significance of restoring an element of the body of Christ that has been lost for centuries.

For over seventeen hundred years of Christian history, God's people have been prohibited from starting their own songs. Instead, professional musicians tell us what to sing, when to sing, and when to stop singing. They tell us when to stand and when to sit down. You and I have been robbed from the privilege of handling the ministry of song as the body of Christ.

In addition, the instruments and the professional singers mask the fact that you and I are horrific at corporate singing. If you removed the song leader, the worship team, or the choir from every church, it would become painfully obvious that most Christian groups do not sing very well together. (This can be remedied, however. And it will be remedied in your group.)

Even in most institutional churches, music is still an instrument of the clergy. The control simply moves from an organ or a piano to a guitar. And we continue to get cut off from managing our own singing. The problem runs very deep.

When most churches that have open-participatory meetings get started, some of the members will ask permission to sing a particular song. To wit, *"Can we sing 'Blessed Assurance'?"* Such a request is simply a symptom of having one's singing controlled by a music leader.

When singing is fully in the hands of the church, we Christians do not ask permission to sing our songs. We boldly lead the singing. It sounds like this: *"Let's sing 'Blessed Assurance,'"* or we just start the song ourselves. Please remind one another that it's your right and privilege as members of the body of Christ to lead your own songs. We don't ask permission to do it. We can all request or start a song.

The Flavor of Christian Songs

Institutional churches have undergone bloody splits over what types of songs to sing in their services. Countless churches have divided over whether to sing the old hymns or to incorporate contemporary choruses—whether to have choirs or worship teams.

Point: The issue of music and singing tends to bring out the flesh.

If you have within you a mind to surrender and forfeit, rather than to push your personal preferences, your new church will gain. If not, it will suffer.

The overriding purpose of this chapter is twofold:

1. To awaken your spiritual instincts so that you may break free from human tradition in the area of worshipping God through song. (Note that a good portion of that tradition is incredibly subtle. A year from now you will look back and see how much of it had a choke hold on you.)

2. To help water the creativity that's resident within your regenerated spirit.

How to Build a Songbook

If every believer had a photographic memory and could sing hundreds of songs by heart, and they could transmit those songs to the minds of visitors who never heard them, then creating a songbook would be unnecessary.

1. I know of two ways to build a songbook. Both have advantages and disadvantages. Consider the following:

A. Loose-leaf notebook format. Everyone in the group purchases an 8.5 x 5.5" loose-leaf notebook. It's a good idea to purchase some extras for guests who will visit you in the future.

Have everyone put his or her name on the front of the notebook. (I assure you, songbooks will be left in meetings.) Also, put a label on the guest songbooks that says something like "Guest Songbook: Please Do Not Take Home." Neglect this, and there's an awfully good chance that someday you will discover that all of your guest songbooks have suddenly disappeared.

The advantage of a loose-leaf notebook is that you can easily add and remove songs. It gives your songbook a front door and a back door. With ease, you can remove songs that you find tiresome and worn out. And you can easily add new ones. As the years pass, your songbook will grow. It will also reflect your spiritual experiences as a believing community.

I've known groups that created a songbook using a loose-leaf notebook approach, but without the actual notebook. The pages were hole punched and three interlocking rings held them together into a little book. A songbook created with this approach is very easy to handle while singing songs standing up.

B. Staple-bound booklet format. Create a songbook using 8.5 x 11" sheets of paper. Print your songs out using landscape mode, one song on the left side and one song on the right side. You will have to number the songs according to the way they will be laid out when all the pages are stapled together. Go to an office-supply store to staple the pages together with a hard-paper cover on it, creating an 8.5 x 5.5" booklet. The advantage of this format is that it's very easy to handle while singing. The disadvantage is that you can't add or remove songs. Thus if you go this route, you may want to revise your songbook every six to twelve months or so. Delete the worn-out and never-sung songs and add fresh ones.

2. Create a starter list of songs. In one of your meetings, make a list of your favorite Christian songs that you would like added to the songbook. It's best if you can find the lyrics, print them out, and make copies for everyone in your group. Most Christian songs can be found on the Web using Google.com. Type in the name of the song and put an ampersand along with the word *lyrics*. It will look like this: *Crown Him with Many Crowns & lyrics*.

3. Appoint someone to be in charge of the songbook. Select someone to be responsible to type up the lyrics of the songs, print them out, make copies, cut the sheets, and hole punch them so that they can be added to everyone's songbook. If you introduce a song to the group, it would be of great help if you could email the lyrics to the person creating the songbook. That way, they only have to copy, paste, and format the song to an 8.5 x 5.5" page, and print it out. (Hopefully, you have someone in your group who is computer savvy.)

4. Learn new songs in your meetings. A suggestion: Every time you meet, each person has both the right and the privilege to introduce one or two songs to the group. Unless everyone in the group decries the song, go ahead and add it to the songbook. There's no harm in doing so. These first six months plus constitute the season for you to learn tons of new songs.

5. Practice your songs. Sing them often. Every six months to a year, have a special meeting where your group votes on which songs to keep in the songbook and which ones to remove. Songs that are rarely sung or just worn out should be deleted. (They can always be reintroduced later on.) It's important that your songbook be kept fresh and up-to-date. Have fun learning your songs. Don't be afraid to laugh at yourselves. Keep everything light.

How to Write a Song

Regarding songwriting, we can learn a great deal from the early Anabaptists. The Anabaptists created their own hymnals. With each hymn, they printed the names of the melodies that were familiar to the people of their day. In other words, the Anabaptists wrote their songs to the tunes of the popular music of their time.

This was a well-known practice of Martin Luther, William Booth, and many others throughout the centuries. Some of our most treasured hymns were written to the tunes of well-known secular songs. "Amazing Grace," "Beautiful Savior," and "How Great Thou Art" are just some of them.

Consequently, if you are not musically inclined or gifted, you can follow the path of your Christian forefathers. Take a contemporary song and redeem it by writing Christian lyrics to the tune.

It's best to use tunes that are popular in your generation. Broadway musicals and children's tunes are always good choices because they tend to be timeless.

Here is how you go about writing a song. Pick a song that can be easily sung a cappella. Obtain the original words and write them down or type them out. (Again, you can search the lyrics for virtually any song that has ever been written using Google.com on the Internet.)

This is imperative: *Accurately count the number of syllables in each stanza.* You can't afford to miss here. Next, overlay your new lyrics using the same number of syllables for each stanza.[1]

What follows is an example of how a song can be written to a popular tune. One of the churches I planted wrote this song to the tune of "Somewhere Over the Rainbow." Note that the line "Somewhere Over the Rainbow" contains seven syllables. The replacement for this

---

1 See "Songwriting Fundamentals" by Dave Byers at www.writingsongs.com/davebyers/tips/songwriting_basics.htm.

line is "My bride, you have been chosen"—seven syllables. A perfect match.

Here's the entire song:

"Kind of My Own Kind"
(Sung to the tune of "Somewhere Over the Rainbow")

(Brothers)
My bride, you have been chosen before time
Blessed with all of your glory
Blameless before my sight

(Sisters)
My Lord, you're all I long for, I need you
All the dreams that I dare to dream
Really are of you

(Brothers) Each day I take you in my arms
(Sisters) And dance with me beyond the stars
(All) Together

(Brothers) I live in you and you in me
(Sisters) Entwined for all eternity
(All) How you complete me

(All)
My Love, I want to give you everything
True love, joy, and devotion
All that you are to me

Beholding you I always find
How truly you are
Kind of my own Kind!

This song was written after a time of spoken ministry on the love relationship between Christ—the Bridegroom—and His church, the bride. It was born out of a spiritual revelation and experience. (Some of that ministry has been transcribed, and it appears in my book *From Eternity to Here.*)

Herein lies an important principle: The most treasured Christian hymns were born out of a new seeing of the Lord or a new encounter with Him. This finds precedent in the psalms. The psalms make up a hymnbook that was birthed out of the spiritual experiences of David and others.

Again, the key to rewriting songs is to count the syllables of the original tune and match them *perfectly* with your new lyrics. If you fail to do this, the song will not match the tempo of the tune, and it will be painfully awkward to sing.

Let me add a few other tips along this line. If a Christian song has a great melody but the words are insipid or not theologically accurate, you can change the words to improve the song. You may even enhance a popular Christian song by adding new stanzas to it or by rewriting some of the lyrics.[2]

Sometimes you will have trouble making a word fit your song because it has too many syllables. There are some shortcuts around this. For instance, hymn writers throughout history have cheated on the word *heaven* by truncating it down to one syllable. They have transformed it into *heav'* or *heav'n*. *Jesus* is two syllables, but it can be easily substituted by *Lord* or *Christ* if you need a one-syllable word to replace it.

---

2   All of the above suggestions assume a knowledge of copyrights. Some songs are protected by copyright laws. I'm not suggesting that you violate such laws. Information about these laws can be found at www.ccli.com.

Writing lyrics to known tunes is a great way to add new songs to your songbook. However, it's rather difficult at first. But with time and practice, it will become much easier.

Tips for Introducing New Songs for Your Songbook
1. I suggest you only introduce songs that meet the following criteria:

- ❧ The song has spiritual depth. What do I mean? Well, compare the lyrics to "I've Got a Home in Gloryland" ("Do Lord") and "Father Abraham" with the lyrics to "When I Survey the Wondrous Cross," and contemplate the difference in spiritual depth.

- ❧ The song accurately reflects your beliefs and vision as a believing community. Example: If you don't believe that the church is a building, then why on earth would you sing songs whose lyrics reflect this notion?

- ❧ The song is Christocentric (meaning, it is Christ-centered and glorifies your Lord). Many Christian songs talk about "God," but they have no reference to Jesus Christ or the riches that are in Him. Christ was the subject of the early Christians' hymns as well as their conversation, their writing, and their preaching. The centrality and supremacy of the Lord Jesus Christ is one of the missing notes in much of modern Christianity. My friend Leonard Sweet calls it JDD—Jesus Deficit Disorder. To neglect the centrality of Christ is to neglect the very meaning of why you exist as a church. It's important, therefore, that most of your songs be Christ-centered.

❧ The song is neither outdated nor dead. Omit time-bound songs that have been dead for many years. By contrast, timeless songs are songs that still have an anointing on them even though they were written hundreds of years ago. Examples of timeless songs are "How Great Thou Art," "All Hail the Power of Jesus' Name," "Amazing Grace," "Crown Him with Many Crowns," "To God Be the Glory," "It Is Well with My Soul," and "When I Survey the Wondrous Cross." Some timeless songs are fairly recent. But they still have an anointing on them when sung today. Examples are "As the Deer," "I Will Enter His Gates," "More Precious Than Silver," and "When I Look into Your Holiness." Examples of time-bound songs that, like the church in Sardis, were once alive but now dead are "Pass It On, Jehovah-Jirah," "His Ways Are Higher Than Mine," and a host of others too numerous to list. Note: Your discernment on which songs to include in

your songbook will change and mature as you
discover the deeper aspects of Christ. Don't get
under bondage. Don't make this into law. Go
with your best judgment.

*2. Be sure to learn the song yourself before you introduce it to the
group.* If you don't know it, don't expect the group to be able to sing
it.

3. Be sure that the song can float a cappella. Some songs can be
sung only with an instrument like a guitar or piano. My advice: Wait
on introducing those types of songs until later when you introduce
musical instruments into your gatherings. Right now, sing songs that
can be easily sung a cappella.

*4. If you write a song and introduce it to the group, be willing to allow
others to improve it.* I've watched some songs be transformed from fair
to stellar simply because the authors were willing to allow others to
tinker with their lyrics. Take that as a gentle encouragement.

*5. If a song has only one stanza, you can enrich the song by adding
more stanzas.* Many of the tunes that have come out of the charismatic
movement are "7-11 songs." That is, they are comprised of seven
lines that are sung eleven times. These songs can be enhanced by
writing more stanzas to them.

6. Consistently be on the hunt for new songs. Christians have
written some of the most beautiful lyrics and tunes known to man.
Find the great ones and use them. If you ever stop learning new
songs, you will get dry. A constant influx of new songs that glorify
the Lord Jesus and express your revelation and experience of Him is
vital to staying spiritually fresh and vibrant.

7. Don't be afraid to restart a song. About 25 percent of the time, when you begin a song a cappella, it will be pitched too high or too low. Instead of enduring through the now-butchered song, stop and restart it again at a singable pitch. Once again, be willing to laugh at yourselves and keep it light.

8. Sing the song several times before moving on to the next one. This will help you to learn each song. It will also help you to worship and/ or praise your Lord through the song as you contemplate the lyrics.

Practical Exercises

- ✤ Appoint someone to be in charge of your songbook.

- ✤ Develop a plan on how to get your songbook started.

CHAPTER 17

BUILDING COMMUNITY

*We humans learn best when in relationship with others
who share a common practice.*

—Margaret Wheatley

The church is a company of people who meet around, under, for, and unto Christ. But it's also a people who share their lives together in Christ.

Biblically speaking, the church is an extended family. In fact, the family is the favorite metaphor that the New Testament authors use to depict the church. For this reason, the biblical writers refer to the men in the church as "brothers" and the women as "sisters."

As I have explained in my book *Reimagining Church*, the *ekklesia* is an earthly echo of the eternal community that exists within the Godhead. God is a communal Being. And we are made in His image. Consequently, we are designed for community. This lays down an important centerpiece for body life. It is critical to develop a communal life in Christ that displays the community of the triune God.

In all the years that I have experienced organic church life, I've made a number of observations as to how communal bonds are formed and strengthened. One of the building blocks of community is rooted in the deep need for Christian men to spend time with other Christian men. The goal is so that a Christian brotherhood can be built.

In like manner, Christian women have an instinctual need to spend time with other Christian women. The goal being that they may be welded together into a spiritual sisterhood.

Amazing things happen when we come together with our own sex around the Lord—things that could never happen if the opposite sex were present.

For instance, a brother may be struggling with a very personal issue. He has a need to share it with his fellow brothers. But he would feel awkward, embarrassed, and inhibited if anyone without a Y chromosome were present.

The same applies to women. Our sisters in Christ have an inimitable way of connecting with their fellow sisters when men are absent. I made this observation almost twenty-one years ago in my first experience of body life. It seems to be written in the bloodstream of the church.

Meetings for Men and Women

I would recommend that the men in the group find a time when they can meet either every week or every other week. I would also recommend that the women meet together every week or every other week. (If you meet every other week, the women should alternate their weeks with the men.) No children should be present during these meetings.

When the sisters meet, your main goal for coming together at this early stage is to share your hearts and have fun together. Talk about your week, your lives, your children, your husbands. Discuss your hopes, your dreams, and your fears. Talk about what you would like to see in your church-life experience together. Talk about the Lord. Have fun with each other. Joke, laugh, play, cry. *Just be yourselves.*

In time, you will feel comfortable enough to share your struggles and difficulties. This is risky business, and it demands courage. But it will come naturally. And when it does, others will be encouraged to do the same. Few things build community as solidly as helping one another cope with real-life struggles.

When the brothers meet, do the same. Feel free to tease one another. And don't make the mistake of taking one another too seriously. Certainly don't take yourself too seriously. Have fun together. If your meeting gets tense, someone should tell a joke to lighten the air.

Gentle teasing is great fun, and it has power to break the ice. Close-knit families are noted for their good-spirited teasing. However, be careful not to allow yourselves to be mean spirited and cruel to one another in the name of teasing. Or worse, to tease about things that are completely untrue without noting that you are "just kidding" at the end of your ribbing.

There's a line between gentle teasing and being demeaning, cruel, belittling, insulting, ridiculing, mocking, and misleading. Using a tease can be a form of character assassination. We have not so learned the lessons of Jesus Christ. Crossing this line actually grieves the Spirit of God. I have seen it destroy Christian brotherhood. It ends up eroding trust between brothers in Christ. Trust and emotional safety cannot be built in such an atmosphere. So tease. But do so in good-spirited fun and stay on the up-and-up.

One of the things you'll want to do in your brothers' meetings is to make sure that the women and the men are having their "overnight meetings" (see next section). You will also want to talk about any needs that are in the group (e.g., a single sister in your group may need help repairing her car, a brother may be out of work and needs financial help, etc.). Your brothers' meetings are also a platform to hash out problems and get the Lord's mind on solutions.

If you can create a safe environment that fosters trust, your brothers' meetings will become extremely important to you. These meetings will eventually become the place where you will find the Lord's mind together. The place where you will feel safe sharing the deepest secrets of your hearts, knowing that they will not leave the room. Brothers' meetings will become one of the safest havens that you will ever know this side of the veil. Sisters' meetings will become the same for the women in the church.

Another thing I would encourage you to do is to begin each of your meetings (both men's and women's meetings) with singing. Open up your gatherings with worship songs to the Lord. Then move into your sharing. I have discovered that a meeting will take on a higher and more spiritual atmosphere if you begin it with worship.

In addition to your weekly or bimonthly meetings for brothers and sisters, I would like to introduce you to another kind of meeting that is extremely helpful for community building. It's the "overnight meeting."

Sisters' Sleepovers

The "sisters' sleepover" can be one of the most exhilarating and unforgettable experiences you will ever have as a Christian woman. Here's how it works: Find a home in which to meet where no males or children are present. (Husbands should watch the children during that weekend.) *This meeting is for women only.* Begin on Saturday morning and go straight through till Sunday afternoon. The church will have no corporate meeting during this weekend.

The sisters' sleepover has one goal in mind: to give the Lord a time when you can be built together as sisters. The object of this meeting is to get to know one another very well in an informal setting of freedom and fun.

Sisters who have had sleepovers have often testified how they felt comfortable enough to share their hearts with their fellow sisters and to receive healing from the Lord as a result. Many wonderful things can happen in a sisters' sleepover that would not ordinarily happen in other contexts. Note: If one or two sisters in your group do not wish to be part of the sleepover, this shouldn't prevent the others from having it. Those sisters who don't wish to sleep overnight should still be encouraged to stay as late as they wish during the first evening.

If the women in your group are open to trying this, I would suggest having this sort of meeting once every two or three months. Here is a list of some things that sisters have done in their sleepovers in the past. Feel free to use some of them. Experiment. And come up with your own ideas:

- Play "Two Truths and a Lie"—each sister writes two true statements and one false statement about herself on a sheet of paper. (Don't write your name on it.) Mix up the papers. Each person draws a paper and reads it aloud. The group must guess who the author is and then guess which statement is the lie.

- Make ice-cream sundaes together. Everyone brings a topping.

- Eat popcorn, drink hot chocolate, and talk the night away.

- Choose "Secret Sisters." Select a name and secretly encourage that sister with notes, cards, Scriptures, etc., for the next three months or so. After three months, reveal yourselves at your next sleepover. Each sister plans something extra special to honor the sister whom she has been encouraging over the last three months. Choose different names and start over if you wish.

- Each sister wears a name tag on her back, but she will not know what name it is. All the names should have the same theme, such as actors and actresses, Bible characters, the men in the group, the women in the group, different occupations, etc. Each sister asks the others questions to try and figure out the name on her back.

❧ Create a skit for the brothers. It can be funny or serious. It might be about your time together as sisters or something you have all freshly learned about the Lord. It can be based on a certain story in Scripture that you act out.

❧ Rent and watch a movie together.

❧ Bake/cook something new together.

❧ Play board games.

❧ Play charades.

❧ Play Pictionary.

❧ Do a white-elephant gift exchange.

❧ Write a song together. Take a long song in the genre of Don McLean's "American Pie." Have the sisters pair off. Each pair rewrites one stanza of the song. Then put the entire song together and sing it to the Lord. Perform the song for the brothers the next time you meet with them.

❧ Answer and discuss some of the ice-melting questions at the end of this chapter.

❧ Plan something special for the brothers. Something that will bless their socks off. One example is to plan a meal for them around a theme. I remember being in a brothers' meeting in the past, and the sisters crashed our meeting. They all paraded into the living room wearing white blouses and black skirts. They escorted us into the backyard where they had decorated a picnic table for us. (We had no idea that they had done this.) Each plate had a rose beside it. The sisters served us a three-course Italian meal they had prepared themselves. While we ate, they surrounded us and sang a song they had written called "That's Agape." It was sung to the tune of "That's Amore." Here are the lyrics:

"That's Agape"
(Sung to the tune of "That's Amore")

Prologue:
In Ekklesia, where Christ is King.
When we see our brothers, here's what we sing:

When the bride seems to shine with a love that's divine,
That's agape.
We see you, we see Christ, we see Christ in your lives,
That's agape.

Tag:
We all sing, glorify the King, Hallelujah.

*Chosen ones, holy men, rising early seeking
   Him,
That's agape.*

*From His side, sanctified, Christ's pure life
   dwells inside,
You are holy.*

*Laying lives down for friends, on our brothers
   we depend,
That's agape.*

*Tag:
When you walk in a dream, but you know
   you're not dreaming, señor, excusame, but you
   see, here in old Floridi ... that's agape!*

Brothers' All-Nighters

In the same way, it's important for Christian men to spend quality time together. So I recommend a two-day all-nighter once every two or three months. The brothers should alternate their months with the sisters' sleepovers. Start Saturday and go through till Sunday afternoon.

No women or children should be present. These meetings are designed to give the Lord an opportunity to build you together as Christian men—as brothers in Christ. Here are some things that brothers have done in their all-nighters in the past:

- Go camping together. Or stay over at one of the brothers' homes.

- Plan a fishing trip.

❧ Eat, joke, share your hearts, and have fun with one another.

❧ Talk about what it means to you to be a brother in the community of the King.

❧ Rent a movie, play games, write a song together to present to the whole group, answer and discuss some of the ice-melting questions at the end of this chapter.

❧ Stage a skit, drama, or play to act out a story found in Scripture. Write the script and plan out each scene. Rehearse it, fine-tune it, then present it to the sisters.

❧ Plan something spectacular for the sisters. Something that will blow their hose off! One example is to prepare a gourmet dinner for them. Include songs to sing for them, a skit, flowers, gifts for each of them, specialized cards that speak of Christ's love for each sister, etc. Remind them of who they are in Christ. Be clever. Be witty. Be silly. Have everyone dress up for the occasion. Your creativity is the limit.

❧ Take turns reading parts of the book *Wild at Heart* by John Eldredge or *The Wild Man's Journey* by Richard Rohr, and discuss practical ways to implement the content.

🌱 Discuss practical ways that the husbands in the church can romance their wives.

🌱 Discuss practical ways that the brothers as a group can be a blessing to the single sisters.

Community Builders for Brothers

The following are things that brothers can do together in a given week:

🌱 Go to the movies or watch a video/DVD together. Then discuss it.

🌱 Go to a sporting event together.

🌱 Go fishing together.

🌱 Play Frisbee golf.

🌱 Go skiing (water or snow).

🌱 Play extreme go-carting.

🌱 Go white-water rafting.

🌱 Go jet-skiing.

🌱 Go skeet shooting.

🌱 Play a game of softball.

🌱 Have a basketball tournament.

- Play tennis-court baseball (use a taped-up whiffle ball and bat).

- Play touch football.

- Go on a canoe trip.

- Play paintball.

- Go surfing.

- Play volleyball.

- Have mock wrestling matches.

- Hold an arm-wrestling tournament.

- Play flashlight tag.

- Help each other work on your automobiles.

- Help one another with lawn work.

- Exercise together.

- Go out to eat together.

- Wash one another's cars.

- Invite one another over for dinner.

- Babysit for a married couple in the group.

- Help one another with "handyman" work around the house.

Community Builders for Sisters

The following are things that sisters can do together in a given week:

- All the sisters gather together to clean another sister's house. Rotate doing this each month until each sister's home has been cleaned by the other sisters.

- Take a sister out to shop for new clothes.

- Send a sister to have a manicure, pedicure, or massage while the rest of you watch her children.

- All the sisters get together for a pampering day where they receive facials, massages, manicures, pedicures, etc.

- Do a personal makeover for one of the sisters.

- Exercise together. Go to the gym and perhaps take a class together.

- Have dinners together.

- Help make scrapbooks for each other.

- Create circle journals that record your spiritual lives in the church.

- Make a recipe book together.

- Babysit for married couples so they can have a date night out.

- Send flowers to a sister randomly or on a special occasion.

- Have lunch together.

- Make dinner for a single sister or take her out to a movie.

- Have a "Sisters Night Out." All the sisters get dressed up and go out to a fancy restaurant and then to the theater to watch a play. (Husbands will send their wives out with a rose. The other sisters will provide a rose for the single sisters.) This is your night to be spectacular together.

- Go walking together—at parks, in the mountains (if you have them), in your neighborhood, etc.

- Each sister takes a turn teaching one another a hobby or craft.

- Go to the beach.

- Go horseback riding.

- Play a game like Bunko.

- Go tubing at a spring.

❧ Plan a "game night" for the whole church where the sisters challenge the brothers and compete with them.

In addition to all of the above, someone should make a phone/email list of everyone in the group. It should also include everyone's birthday, including the children's. Pass this list out to everyone. Find a way to celebrate everyone's birthday. A good idea is for each member who has a birthday to share their reflections over the past year. Celebrate when someone gets a promotion, a new job, or graduates. Valentine's Day is a great opportunity for the men in the church—as a group—to bless the women. And vice versa.

All of these things help to nurture and develop a communal life in Jesus Christ. Again, right now your main goal is to get to know one another in an atmosphere of informality, fun, and freedom—and lots of laughter. Community cannot be built without these ingredients. This is the foundation you need for authentic church life to be born.

Ice-Melting Questions

The following are questions that can be asked in your group to help melt the ice with one another. Feel free to use some of these during your overnight meetings or any other time that your group gathers together:

❧ What was the most significant thing that happened to you last week?

- Name something that people will be surprised to find out about you.

- Describe your first job.

- What is the best gift you received as a child?

- Name some traditions that your family regularly observes.

- What is your dream job?

- Where did you grow up? Describe it.

- Suppose you could choose one famous person alive today and they would come to Christ. Who would you choose and why?

- What places have you traveled to?

- What would you like to accomplish over the next five years?

- Imagine that you woke up tomorrow morning with a new ability or skill. What would it be?

- What do you wish to do after you retire?

- If you could spend an entire day with any human being alive today, who would it be and why?

- Name a major goal you have for your life.

- What is the best compliment you have ever received?

- Share two of your greatest strengths.

- Share a dream (aspiration) that you have which has not yet come to pass.

- What do you usually do with gifts that you do not particularly like?

- Name your two favorite movies. Why are they your favorites?

- What is your favorite television show of all time? Why is it your favorite?

- When you were a child, what did you want your career to be?

- What is your favorite place to vacation?

- What is the best trip you have ever taken?

- What two foods do you not care for at all?

- What are your two favorite dishes?

- What is your favorite dessert?

- What is your favorite junk food?

- Tell us about your first vehicle.

❧ What was the best thing that happened to you last year?

❧ What does your name mean and/or who were you named after?

Practical Exercises

❧ Decide on a day, a time, and a place to have your brothers' meetings.

❧ Decide on a day, a time, and a place to have your sisters' meetings.

❧ Using your calendar, pick a weekend when (and where) the women will have their first sleepover.

❧ Using your calendar, pick a weekend when (and where) the men will have their first all-nighter.

CHAPTER 18

TWELVE ESSENTIAL INGREDIENTS

> *As the Preacher of Ecclesiastes saw, "There is a time to break down, and a time to build up ... a time to keep silence and a time to speak." And the second Reformation, if it comes, will be distinguished from the first by the fact that it is a time of reticence, of stripping down, of traveling light. The church will go through its baggage and discover how much it can better do without, alike in doctrine and in organization.*

—John A. T. Robinson

The following ingredients were discovered as I and others navigated the uncommon terrain of experiencing the headship of Jesus Christ without a clergy. I pass them on to you with the hopes that your new church plant will find them to be as helpful as I have.

1. Lower your expectations. Understand that the road to body life is paved with difficulty. It's fraught with obstacles, challenges, and hazards. Sometimes you will disappoint and fail one another. This is part of the package of churching with human beings. So lower your expectations, and don't expect perfection from your sisters and brothers in Christ—let alone from yourself.

2. It is unwise and counterproductive to attack an idea unless you have one that can top it. Stated differently: Unless you can improve upon someone else's idea or practice, do not criticize it.

3. If you suggest an idea, take responsibility to carry it out. In other words, if you ever find yourself saying to the group, "Why don't we do such and such," understand that you have just volunteered yourself to be the person to spearhead it.

4. Never be afraid of being creative. Arm yourselves with a spirit of exploration, experimentation, and discovery. Get used to doing things you've never heard or dreamed of doing. Meeting without a clergy is a pioneering endeavor. There are many discoveries to be made along the journey that will be of benefit to others who will also put their hands to this plow.

5. It is acceptable to fail. Do not fear making mistakes, but seek to learn from them. It's far better to fail than not to try at all. It is nobler to step out of the boat and sink than it is to stay in the boat due to fear of failure.

6. Guard against the tendency to be legalistic. Avoid putting your own personal convictions and standards of Christian conduct upon the other members of the group. (I've written an entire chapter on this very issue in my free ebook, *Rethinking the Will of God.*[1] I suggest that

---

1   See chapter 4 of the ebook. You may freely download it at www.ptmin.org/rethinkingthewill.pdf.

your group read that chapter together at some point. It could very well save your new church from a painful split down the road.)

7. If someone has a practical idea for the group that you have never tried, tilt hard toward saying yes to them. Reserve the word *no* for ideas that violate your conscience or if they put the group back under religious bondage or the old wineskin. It's crucial that you support one another.

8. If you miss a meeting, it's your responsibility to find out when and where the next meeting will take place. It's also your responsibility to find out what the group will be doing for the next meeting so that you can prepare for it.

9. Understand and accept the two basic personality types in the church: the extrovert and the introvert. Extroverts are the outgoing, fearless, have-too-much-to-say talkers. Some of them are chatterboxes that don't possess an off switch.

Introverts are the inward, timid, I'd-rather-sit-and-watch personalities. It's difficult for them to share and participate. It won't take you long to identify the extroverts and the introverts. The extroverts tend to overparticipate, and the introverts tend to underparticipate. This is normal. The challenge is for both of these personalities to understand their personality type and let the Lord move them toward the opposite direction.

If you're an overparticipating extrovert, learn to restrain yourself and not talk so much. If you're an underparticipating introvert, stretch yourself to share more. Both of you must be willing to die a bit to your basic natures.

Note: In most cases, introverts are willing to share. But they often have to be asked to share their thoughts. Please don't forget that. Also, if a quiet person offers an idea or suggestion, pay close attention to what they have to say and give it weight.

10. The following is on equal par with the law and the prophets. The single women in your church have no husbands. Special attention should be given to them by the married couples and by the brothers *as a group*. Single sisters struggle with loneliness a great deal. Thus, married couples should make it a habit of including them for dinners, occasional movies, etc. Their home/car maintenance needs should be looked after by the brothers as a group also.

11. If someone in your group has a pet doctrine or a theological hobbyhorse that they continue to peddle in your meetings, detracting everyone else from Christ, here's something to try. Set aside a special meeting (one event) during the week where this person can present their doctrine to the group without interruption.

Make an agreement ahead of time. When this person has shared his or her heart and he or she is finished, the group will react to it. If the person has convinced everyone with his or her doctrine, then he or she must agree to no longer bring it up during your meetings. Everyone is convinced, so there's no need. If the person doesn't convince everyone, then he or she must agree to stop talking about it altogether.

Remember, at this stage, your meetings are centered on getting to know one another in the Lord. They are not to be used as a platform to expound your favorite doctrine. I exhort you, therefore, to leave your specialized doctrines at the door and do not monopolize the church with them.

12. Remember that organic church life is a lot like marriage. The first six months to a year is your honeymoon period. So enjoy it right now.

Reasonable Expectations

In closing, if you will give the lessons outlined in this section a chance, I expect the following to happen in time:

- ❧ The chains of religious bondage will begin to fall off your wrists.

- ❧ You will begin to taste the freedom that was purchased by Christ.

- ❧ You will feel more comfortable sharing in a gathering of believers.

- ❧ The Christian life will be more fun to you than it has been in the past. You will smile more.

- ❧ You will begin to develop a new mind-set about your Lord and about the Christian walk.

- ❧ You will no longer be boxed into denominational or institutional thinking.

- ❧ The New Testament will become a new book to you.

- ❧ You will care for and appreciate the people in the group more than you did when you first met them. In fact, you may even view them as your real brothers and sisters.

- ❧ Your hunger and desire for the Lord will increase.

- ✤ You will become more "normal" and less religious than when you first began this journey.

- ✤ You will begin to discover just how influenced you were by a religious mind-set. And you will start to realize just how deep that rabbit hole goes.

Remember, the lessons in this section have but one goal: *to move you toward meetings and community life that are under the headship of the Lord Jesus Christ.* It takes time to get there. So be patient. Have fun, and relish the ride.

The Lord's blessing be upon you as you embark on this new adventure.

In the next section, we'll explore the health and development of an organic church.

PART FOUR
PULLING THE WEEDS—
HEALTH AND DEVELOPMENT

CHAPTER 19

THE GROWTH STAGES OF AN ORGANIC CHURCH

Like newborn babies, crave pure spiritual milk, so that
by it you may grow up in your salvation.

—Peter in 1 Peter 2:2

One of my many flaws is my inability to multitask. I'm keenly aware that most men have a hard time multitasking. But in my case, it's a terminal condition (this is sober autobiography). If you are ever a passenger in an automobile that I'm driving, don't engage me in a conversation. It may result in me inadvertently taking you to Mexico!

The good side of this shortcoming is that when I do concentrate on something, such as a conversation, I can listen to it on many different levels. So, like most human deficiencies, there's some compensation.

One of the things I've given my concentration to over the years is how an organic church grows, develops, lives, and dies.

My quest for the church after God's own heart has led me to raise some critical questions on this score. Such as: What are the necessary ingredients that make for a healthy, vibrant church that reflects the biblical vision of the body of Christ? Why do so many nontraditional churches dissolve? What are the stages that an organic church will pass through, and what should we know about each one?

Again, many churches that set out to gather outside traditional church structures have a short shelf life. This has led many people to conclude that being church the way the early Christians were simply doesn't work in our day. They've concluded that we *must* have an institutional structure to keep everything afloat.

I've grappled with this particular argument in my other volumes, so I won't rehearse my responses here. Instead, I would like to tackle what my journey has taught me regarding the stages of growth that an organic church will pass through.

Based on what I've seen over the last two decades, I believe that every group of Christians who leaves the institutional church and seeks to gather under the headship of Christ in an organic way will ultimately end up in one of four places. I call these places "destinies." Let's briefly look at each one, moving from worst to best.

Four Destinies

1. Disintegration. Over a period of time, many organic churches fall apart. They fall apart for different reasons. Most often it's due to an internal conflict—be it a personality conflict, a doctrinal conflict, or a conflict in practice. The group lacks the spiritual resources and maturity to handle the conflict, so it self-destructs. When this happens, the damage can be devastating.

I've met a number of casualties of church life who have grown sour on the whole idea. They put their hands in the fire and got burned badly. They are now living in a spiritual wasteland, still licking their wounds. The idea of getting close to other Christians mortifies them. The mantra they fly under is: "I've tried meeting like that once, and it just doesn't work."

Regrettably, many of these battle-scarred souls will be spiritually deformed for the rest of their lives. Of course, they can receive the Lord's healing if they choose to and move on toward fulfilling His purpose.

Another reason for disintegration is "rustout." When a church rusts out, the members get bored with doing the same thing over and over again. They get caught in the tyranny of the routine. As my friend Hal Miller likes to say, "Everything is prone to becoming first mundane, then rote, then unimportant." No fresh input is given to the church, and everyone is ready to throw in the towel. Attendance to meetings grows progressively poorer until hardly anyone shows up. Rustout usually happens when a church doesn't receive the blessing of extralocal help, which aids it in defying entropy.

Burnout is another reason for disintegration. This usually happens when an overzealous Christian worker is not sensitive to the needs of a church and tries to push his vision on the members through natural means. Church life moves at a blistering pace without any breaks. The members are cooking with all burners set to high. They eventually wear down from the constant fever pitch and finally burn out. They become so exhausted that the mere thought of a meeting becomes distasteful.

2. Institutionalization. Someone from within the group rises to become its leader. In most cases, this person denies that they are leading the group. Yet if you listen carefully to their rhetoric, it becomes apparent. One dead giveaway is when you hear someone say something like "I've really been trying hard to get them [meaning the church] to see such and such and to do such and such."

The net effect is that the rest of the group grows to look to, depend upon, and passively allow the untitled local leader to do most or all of the ministry. A clergy is present, though it's trying hard to fly under the radar. (This can also take the form of a group of elders who end up controlling the church.)

3. Corporate paralysis. Churches that face this destiny have gone through a number of painful conflicts together. The members keep meeting because it's the right thing to do, but they are handcuffed from making decisions together. They don't want to throw in the towel and lose what they have built so they enter into a corporate paralysis. Meaningful conversations are viewed as exercises in brinkmanship. The church is held together by tissue paper. Everyone tiptoes on pins and needles out of fear that they will offend someone and detonate a bomb. This state can go on for many years without resolve.

4. Spiritual progress. No church ever "arrives." Each one is a story in progress. But those that are making spiritual headway are moving steadily toward the Lord and His eternal purpose.

Conflicts come and go, crises are experienced, but the church survives them all and becomes stronger as a result. The members are being "built together" (to borrow Paul's language), and God is getting what He wants: a bride, a body, a building, and a family—a corporate expression of His glorious Son. Through all the spilling of sweat and blood, coupled with the turmoil that comes with Christian community, the character of Christ is being formed within the members, individually and corporately. And Jesus has a place to lay His head.[1]

A famous philosopher once said, "What doesn't kill you makes you stronger." I like to say that when it comes to body life, whatever makes you stronger kills you. So if you're not willing to die to yourself, the experience of the body of Christ is simply not for you.

Four Stages of Development

As with any life-form, organic churches pass through various stages of growth. In my experience, those stages follow a common pattern.

The first stage is the *honeymoon period.* This is where everything is beautiful. At least it looks that way at first blush. The members experience an uncommon freedom. Their fellowship is sweet and rich. They are enjoying a newfound joy, life, and liberty in Christ. They even *think* they're falling in love with one another. It's a wonderful experience, indeed.

Not every church has a honeymoon period. I've watched some that were born straight into fire. But most will experience a honeymoon. And as surely as the sun will go down tonight, the honeymoon will end. It will destruct. I've never seen a church enjoy a honeymoon perpetually. It will come to an end. And it will lead to stage two—*crisis.*

Something is going to happen that will throw the group into a panic. In his classic book *Life Together*, Dietrich Bonhoeffer uses the

---

1   For details, see the free ebook *Bethany:* www.ptmin.org/bethany.pdf.

word *crisis* to refer to an intense trial that a Christian community faces. I can't think of a better word to describe it.

I've watched so many church crises that I've lost count. Some are mild. Others are traumatic. Still others are blood up to the horse's bit. It's at this point that the group faces a fork in the road. It will either self-destruct, or it will survive the crisis and move on to stage three.

Stage three is the *experience of the cross.* Every crisis is designed to lead us straight to the cross of Christ. It's designed to force us on the horns of this dilemma: Will you die? Will you lose? Will you surrender?

That doesn't mean leaving the group. Nor does it mean fighting for what you feel is the right course of action. It means laying your life down in the midst of the church and handing the situation completely over to the Lord.

Please note: For some people (usually those who are more passive), dying may mean boldly expressing what you believe to be the will of God. For others (usually the strong-willed), it means taking your hands off the situation and surrendering to the mind of the group.

If some aren't willing to die to everything—their opinions, their agendas, their gifts, their ministries, their ideas, their natural temperaments—the church will not survive the crisis.

If you forget everything else in this book, please do not forget this. Organic church life is the most glorious experience a Christian can know. But it does not work, and it will not work, unless you are willing to embrace the cross.

Herein lies an unchanging truth: If you focus on the church, you will get division. But if you focus on Christ and embrace His cross, you will get the church.

If a church successfully bears the cross through the crisis, the church will enter into stage four—*tested body life*. Here's what it looks like: The love the brothers and sisters have for one another has passed through fire. It has matured. The saints realize that they never really *fell* in love with one another; they *climbed* to it. Body life is now deeper and richer than it was during the honeymoon stage. Members will fall on a grenade for one another. They begin to experience the words of Jesus: "Greater love has no one than this, than to lay down one's life for his friends" (John 15:13 NKJV).

Yet the process doesn't stop there. A church will cycle through stages two, three, and four as the years roll by. Each stage is very much like a season. The end in view is the growth of the church into the full image of Christ. Or what Paul called "coming unto full stature" (Eph. 4:13).

The Ministries of Jesus Christ

A good model for understanding the stages of church life is that of the three chief ministries of Jesus Christ—Prophet, Priest, and King. There are the prophetic stage, the priestly stage, and the kingship stage.

The honeymoon stage can be likened to the prophetic ministry of Christ. Prophets are seers. They possess spiritual sight. During the prophetic stage, God's people are given a fresh vision of Christ and His body. That vision is meant to grow in them. It should be watered, fertilized, and nourished. Out of such vision comes the life of the church.

But just as the honeymoon period ends, so does the prophetic stage. The prophetic stage is followed by the priestly stage. What are priests known for? *Sacrifice and death.* The ministry of the priest is to minister at the altar. His ministry is one of sacrifice. This corresponds to church crisis and the cross.

In the priestly stage, the vision is tested through suffering. The Lord's object here is to move the vision from revelation to reality. So this stage involves the crises of church life and the cross that comes with it. The fire comes to test the vision.

Following the priestly stage is the kingship stage. If the Lord gains some ground in the members of the church during the priestly stage, He will be able to use them in the work of His kingdom. The church now begins to impact spiritual powers in unseen realms. A church cannot move into the kingship stage without first experiencing the prophetic and priestly stages.

I think Joseph in the Old Testament beautifully depicts all three stages. God gave Joseph a wonderful and powerful vision. Afterward, his brothers became envious of him. So much so that they tried to take his life. Joseph met the fire and the cross, and it was his own brethren who handed both to him. The wonderful prophetic vision that he received turned into a priestly encounter of great suffering.

Joseph's brethren threw him into a pit and left him for dead. Later, he was imprisoned in a dungeon, falsely accused of committing a gross sin for which he was almost decapitated. I love how the psalms describe Joseph's story:

> *He sent a man before them—Joseph—who was sold as a slave. They hurt his feet with fetters, he was laid in irons. Until the time that his word came to pass, the word of the LORD tested him. The king sent and*

released him, the ruler of the people let him go free.
He made him lord of his house, and ruler of all his
possessions. (Ps. 105:17–21 NKJV)

After much suffering, the vision that Joseph originally received proved true. The prophetic word came to pass. It wasn't a pipe dream after all. Joseph became ruler over Egypt. He entered into the kingship stage.

Note the words of the psalmist: "The word of the LORD tested him." There are thunder and lightning in those words. If you set out to gather in an organic way, the word of the Lord *will* test you. It will try you. The vision for the restoration of God's house will be sorely tested in your life.

And when that moment arrives, you will be tempted to think to yourself: *Is this vision real? … Maybe it worked in the first century, but it doesn't seem to work today.… Is this high and lofty goal really worth the struggle?*

When such thoughts cross your mind, I have but two words for you: *Remember Joseph.*

CHAPTER 20

THE SEASONS OF AN ORGANIC CHURCH

There is a time for everything, and a season for every activity under heaven.

—Solomon in Ecclesiastes 3:1

When I was a young believer, someone told me that one of the reasons why God created the physical seasons was to illustrate the spiritual seasons that a Christian will pass through in his or her life.

After living in organic church life for a while, I came to believe that the earthly seasons represent not only the spiritual seasons of a Christian's life, but that they also represent the spiritual seasons that an organic church will pass through.

As long as I've been gathering in such churches, this has held true. The seasons come and go like clockwork. Genesis 8:22 says, "While the earth remains, seedtime and harvest, cold and heat, winter and summer, and day and night shall not cease" (NKJV).

Jesus talked a lot about the significance of seasons (Matt. 21:41, 45; Luke 12:42; 21:30; John 4:35; 5:35). Paul told his young apprentice Timothy to "be prepared in season and out of season" (2 Tim. 4:2). To borrow the title of Robert Bolt's play about Sir Thomas More, Timothy was to be "a man for all seasons." A man who can stand in the face of every season—great, good, bad, horrible, unmentionable—and not to be moved.

Paul was such a man. Consider his own description of the seasons that he passed through during his ministry:

> *Rather, as servants of God we commend ourselves in every way: in great endurance; in troubles, hardships and distresses; in beatings, imprisonments and riots; in hard work, sleepless nights and hunger; in purity, understanding, patience and kindness; in the Holy Spirit and in sincere love ... known, yet regarded as unknown; dying, and yet we live on; beaten, and yet not killed.... I know what it is to be in need, and I know what it is to have plenty. I have learned the secret of being content in any and every situation, whether well fed or hungry, whether living in plenty or in want. (2 Cor. 6:4–6, 9; Phil. 4:12)*

Like Paul and Timothy, every church is to be "a person for all seasons."

The typical institutional church doesn't pass through seasons because it's tied to a ritual that continues unmoved every week of every month of every year. Consequently, the spiritual temperature of a traditional congregation is hidden underneath the ritual. The performers perform, and the congregation watches, regardless of either's spiritual condition.

One of the wisest men who ever lived taught us well about the different seasons of life. He wrote,

> *There is a time for everything, and a season for every activity under heaven: a time to be born and a time to die, a time to plant and a time to uproot, a time to kill and a time to heal, a time to tear down and a time to build, a time to weep and a time to laugh, a time to mourn and a time to dance, a time to scatter stones and a time to gather them, a time to embrace and a time to refrain, a time to search and a time to give up, a time to keep and a time to throw away, a time to tear and a time to mend, a time to be silent and a time to speak, a time to love and a time to hate, a time for war and a time for peace. (Eccl. 3:1–8)*

What's true in the natural realm is also true in the spiritual realm.

At bottom, a season means a change. As fallen creatures, we don't like change very much. We fall into ruts and routines rather easily. We're bent that way. But science teaches us that all living things must grow or else they die. And growth means change.

For this reason, it's important that a church always maintains a spirit of exploration, experimentation, and discovery. I've learned that if you don't have variety in your church life, you will grow stale. There is an infinite number of ways to express the Lord, there is an infinite number of ways to explore Him, and there is an infinite number of ways to meet under His headship. And all have their due season.

In temperate and polar regions, four seasons are recognized: spring, summer, fall, and winter. In tropical and subtropical regions, only two are recognized: the wet season and the dry season.

We can understand the life of an organic church by examining all six seasons. The seasons of a church, however, do not move in linear progression. They are rhythmic, yet random. They can't be predicted or charted. So the weather channel is no help to us here. In my experience, what follows are the various seasons that an organic church will experience at one time or another. The order doesn't imply any particular priority or any particular order.

Springtime

The springtide of church life is the season of growth. It's the season of rebirth, offspring, and bearing fruit. (In ancient Israel, the spring harvest yielded barley and wheat.) The spring is analogous to the season of outreach. New converts are brought into the church at this time.

If you study the book of Acts carefully, you'll discover that the early church had seasons of outreach. It also had seasons of inreach.

I believe that evangelism needs to be reengineered in our day. Instead of seeking to give people "the plan of salvation" or taking them down "the Roman's road," people in our postmodern society are much more receptive to hear one's personal story about their journey with God.

In addition, people are more receptive when the gospel is enacted before their eyes by action rather than proclaimed by words only. This is especially true in the West where the common person has been desensitized to the Christian message. People are far more impressed with what you do rather than what you say.

In my late teens and early twenties, I experimented with all forms of evangelism. This included door-to-door witnessing, passing out tracts, street preaching, survey evangelism, on-campus witnessing, and the like.

I made one telling discovery in all of it: *They were all highly ineffective.*

The most effective forms of outreach involved demonstrating the gospel in concrete ways. Such as being a genuine friend to unbelievers, caring for the poor, standing up for the oppressed, comforting the afflicted, and engaging in various forms of social concern.

If you examine the life of Jesus while He was on earth, you'll quickly discover that He was deeply concerned with caring for the sick and championing the causes of the poor and oppressed. The life of Christ that indwells the church still moves in that direction, for He is "the same yesterday and today and forever" (Heb. 13:8).

For that reason, a church acting as Christ's physical presence by visible acts of love, compassion, and concern for others is the most effective way to show Jesus to the lost. When the church moves outside the four walls of a building, she becomes the greatest evangelist the world has ever seen.

Another important lesson I learned is that if you're crawling as a newborn church, that's not the time to begin evangelizing. A bundle of new converts with all of their personal problems intact will add three thousand pounds of weight to a newly born organic church. I've seen a number of churches run out of gas because their main purpose for existing was evangelism. They didn't have the spiritual maturity or the resources to handle the new converts, so the church eventually went belly up.

Evangelism can be a horrible mistress. It has the potential to tax and drain a church of its spiritual and physical energy. For that reason, evangelism and outreach ought to be done "in season" rather than as an ongoing program of the church.

I realize that the above recommendation cuts against the grain of modern evangelical thinking. But in my observation, those churches that exist for evangelism tend to be spiritually shallow. Outreach and numerical building are important, but so are inreach and spiritual building. And there's a season for each.

Recognizing that there are seasons for evangelism (outreach) and seasons for spiritual building (inreach) rescues us from fruitless either/or debates over whether the church should focus on evangelism or spiritual building. Understanding the seasonal nature of the church resolves this problem because it's a fresh approach to the question. The question no longer becomes either/or. It rather shifts to when and how.

Summertime, Fall, and Winter

Summer is the season of spiritual building (inreach). It's the sunshine of church life. During this season, the church is firing on all cylinders. The Lord's love is being experienced by the believers in a profound way. The members are maturing in their passion for Christ and in their devotion to one another. (Those two are always connected.)

Fall is the season of prayer. While each individual Christian ought to maintain a regular, steady prayer life, the church will pass through seasons of corporate prayer where she will prepare herself for the winter. This means that everyone in the church will meet together regularly for prayer over a specific matter.

I've been a part of numerous traditional churches that had a regular prayer meeting every week of every month of every year. Without exception, I found all of them to be perfunctory and wooden. A thorough reading of the book of Acts will show that the prayer ministry of the church is seasonal. The church has instincts. She can sense the change in the spiritual atmosphere. She can discern when she's entering into a new season of corporate prayer and when that season has ended.

Winter is the season of sorrow. During a spiritual winter, the spirit of the church starves for color. A church can't always live up in the heavens. It must also experience the cold chill of winter sadness. The body of Christ is not only the treasure, it's also the earthen vessel. The winter is the season of weeping, brokenheartedness, and discouragement.

In my early years as a Christian, I was part of a movement that taught that there was no such thing as a winter in a Christian's life. Discouragement and sadness were things that Christians should resist. And so the people in this movement always tried to keep smiling, never showing any negative emotions. (Some of them cracked under the pressure.)

However, Paul's words in 2 Corinthians helped me to see that the winter season is in fact of God. Paul writes, "For we do not want you to be ignorant, brethren, of our trouble which came to us in Asia: that we were burdened beyond measure, above strength, so that we despaired even of life" (1:8 NKJV).

Paul, the great apostle of Jesus Christ "despaired of life." What a relief that was for me. For I will admit that I sometimes get discouraged. And I've even caught myself complaining. Indeed, we Christians possess the treasure of heavenly joy. But we are living in a fantasy world to deny that this treasure is contained within a clay vessel that experiences the full gamut of human emotions (2 Cor. 4:7ff.).

Winters are difficult, but they exist for the maturity of the church. The winter finally does pass, and the sun does reemerge. Thank God.

We Christians are not stoics. We don't act as though we lack emotions. Job and King David were very open and forthright about their negative feelings, and God didn't condemn them for it. They expressed their discouragement, befuddlement, and perplexity to the Lord as well as to their friends—openly and honestly.

Christians need a safe place where they can express such pain. The church of the Lord Jesus Christ is that very place. When a believer is carrying pain in some area of life, and he or she is sharing that pain with others, he or she should not be callously told, "What are you doing under your circumstances? You have been raised with Christ to heavenly places!"

It's bad enough to go through a painful experience. It's infinitely worse to be blamed or scolded for hurting over it. Paul exhorts the Christians in Rome to "rejoice with those who rejoice, and weep with those who weep" (Rom. 12:15 NKJV). This is the church's DNA at work. There's a season for rejoicing, and there's a season for weeping. And the church lives through both.

Dry Spells and Natural Disasters

The dry spell is the spiritual drought. During this season, the church's throat becomes parched, and her eyes are filled with sand. The meetings are dull and lifeless. Everyone feels as though they are going through the motions. There's a dearth of joy, excitement, and fervor. Songs that once moved the saints to tears no longer touch their hearts. What's happening? You've entered into the dry spell.

To borrow the language of the spiritual writers of the past, the dry spell is "the dry well," "the dark night," "the cloud of unknowing." Death appears everywhere. God has gone on vacation.

Interestingly, there will always be one or two people who feel that the church is *always* in a dry spell. This is simply a reflection of their temperaments. Such people are perfectionists with unrealistic expectations. They always overshoot the goal.

But when a church is passing through a real dry spell, everyone is aware of it (except for the super oblivious—and most churches have at least one or two of those creatures running around).

One of the greatest lessons I learned in my spiritual walk is that God is the author of dry spells. He plans them. He creates them. He brings them. And He eventually removes them.

Our Lord authors dry spells as much as He authors wet spells. He engineers both of them. Those who are of a Pentecostal/charismatic background may be tempted to call the dry season a work of the Devil. But it's not.

It's during the dry spells that most church splits occur. When the river runs dry, the rocks begin to show. When the water recedes, the bottom begins to appear. Moths are attracted to light. But when the lightbulb goes out, they flee in a royal hurry.

Do you know what God is doing during a dry spell? He's searching us out. He's asking the acute question "Do you want Me only during the good times, or do you want Me in the dry times also?"

The church will grow numerically in a wet spell, but it will lose people during a dry spell. Yet the greatest spiritual growth often takes place during the dry spell. But that growth is imperceptible. The dry spell is the season when the deeper lessons of the Christian life are learned.

The church needs dry spells. They are part of the Christian life.

Everyone's devotion to the Lord and to one another is tried during the dry spell. Those who are in the church for what they are getting out of it usually head for the door. The dry spell is God's way of shaking out the fence-sitters. It's the Lord's winnowing tool. It weeds out those who are worshipping the Creator of the universe from those who are worshipping a Cosmic Sugar Daddy. Dry spells separate those who are loyal to the God of blessing from those who are loyal to the blessings of God.

In a word, dry spells are designed to purify our love.

Interestingly, a dry spell can usually be broken. But sometimes it can't. And at such times, the church has but one option: Batten down the hatches, hunker down, and walk through it. Blessed is the church that can ride out the dry spell.

That brings us to the natural disaster. This is a crisis in the life of the church. It's the spiritual hurricane, tornado, earthquake, avalanche, or wildfire.

What's an example of a crisis? Read the New Testament, and look at every letter that Paul penned to a church (excepting Ephesians). In all of them, Paul is addressing a church in crisis. Something is threatening the life of the body. Peter's first two letters and James' letter were also written to churches in crises.

Perhaps Paul had in mind the natural disaster of church life when he talked about "the evil day" of satanic assault, against which the church is to take her stand (Eph. 6:13 NKJV).

Here's my definition of a crisis: *a difficult and challenging opportunity to discover the Lord Jesus Christ in a new way.* To view a crisis through any other lens is to see it from the wrong mountain. Crises will come. It's how we react to them that will determine if the Lord is going to gain more territory in us or if the church will sign its own death warrant. There are three very wise things to do during a crisis: Cling to Jesus Christ, stand against God's enemy, and die to yourself. A crisis is a terrible thing to waste.

The Wet Spell

The wet spell is the season when body life is running at high tide. There's a lot of excitement, joy, and life. The Lord is revealing Himself in new ways, and everyone feels like they've just met Him all over again.

Let's go back in time for a moment. Do you remember when you became a Christian? Do you remember how simple it was? How pure it was? How your heart overflowed with joy and peace?

But then something happened, didn't it? Things started to get complicated. You started "going to church," hearing sermons, and doing Bible studies. And suddenly, the simplicity, the purity, the excitement, and the joy of knowing Jesus Christ melted away.

Well, imagine an entire church "just meeting the Lord" all over again and living out of the joy of their salvation together. Visitors come and their breath is stolen by the sight of Christ in His church. The love is undeniable, the reality is unmistakable, the joy is contagious, the excitement is real, and God's presence is evident. This is the wet spell of organic church life. The church grows numerically the most in this season, and without much effort. It's during the wet spells that Jesus Christ wins the hearts of many.

Sometimes a church may experience a super wet spell, or in modern parlance, a "revival." This is when the water of God's life is running thirty feet high. It's a divine visitation. A riptide of God's Spirit. A gully-washer of spiritual refreshing. The saints gather together for meetings, and no one wants to leave. You can say the name "Jesus," and people get converted.

The day of Pentecost was such a time.

Fortunately, God will not allow a church to stay in the season of revival for very long. The reason: It will tax your physical body to the point of sickness. If a super wet spell continues unabated, God's people will burn out like a cinder. For that reason, revivals come in spurts. The greatest revivals in history had life spans of about four years. I don't think that's a coincidence.

Conclusion

The church of the living God ought to live above seasons. She doesn't wait for revival. Instead, she pursues her Lord even when there is no wind in the mulberry bush. She plows forward with or without wet spells. She marches on outside of springtides. She makes strides during the winters, amid the dry spells, and through the disasters.

She is a woman for all seasons.

In the Old Testament, God set forth the qualifications for the priesthood. If a man had certain defects, he could not serve as a priest. One of them was a flat nose (Lev. 21:18 KJV). A priest had to have a working sense of smell in order to be useful to God.

Throughout the Scriptures, in the Song of Solomon especially, the nose represents spiritual discernment. The ability to smell (physically) represents the ability to discern (spiritually).

An organic church that's mature and growing in Christ will be able to discern the season it is in. It will have a spiritual nose to smell the beginning of a season as well as the end of one. And such discernment is a vital element in its growth.

CHAPTER 21

THE DISEASES OF AN ORGANIC CHURCH I

These are the words of him who holds the seven spirits
of God and the seven stars. I know your deeds; you
have a reputation of being alive, but you are dead.

—Jesus in Revelation 3:1

Since it's possible to acquire a terminal illness unknowingly, many researchers say that the best prevention against certain diseases is early detection. And early detection requires periodic physical exams.

The New Testament repeatedly envisions the church as the body of Christ. Paul spins the body image again and again to describe the *ekklesia*. For Paul, the church is like a physical body. As such, it's a living, breathing, vital organism. It's born. It experiences growth spurts and growth pains. And it passes through specific stages of development.

To put a finer point on it, a church's physical condition can range from healthy to being admitted to the spiritual IC unit (barely alive). Since the church is a living organism, it can contract spiritual disease.

As I've already shared, many organic churches expire within two years. Some, however, keep on meeting even though they are living in the precincts of death (Rev. 3:1). In both cases, the church dies from a fatal illness. Consequently, if a church doesn't know how to build a healthy immune system, it stands wide open for serious sickness.

In this chapter and the next, I would like to introduce you to four common diseases that afflict organic churches.

Please note that I'm not speaking as a theoretician. I've simply watched these diseases afflict such churches for almost two decades. The good news is that none of these diseases is hopelessly terminal. All have a cure. The bad news is that without preventative maintenance and early detection, the chances for survival are slim to none.

As we explore each disease, I'll be spinning a lot of medical terminology, building upon Paul's body metaphor. I'll also be employing a few nonbiblical terms to make specific points. The four diseases are: koinonitis, spiritual myopia, spiritual dwarfism, and hyperpneumia.

Koinonitis

The leading cause of death among organic churches is koinonitis.[1] Koinonitis is a spin-off from the Greek word *koinonia,* which means fellowship.

Speaking of the church in Jerusalem, Luke reports, "And they continued steadfastly in the apostles' doctrine and fellowship [*koinonia*],

1   I owe some of the language in this section to John Butler and Peter Wagner.

in the breaking of bread, and in prayers" (Acts 2:42 NKJV). *Koinonia* is the corporate experience of God Himself. It's the sharing of His life.

You cannot experience *koinonia* by yourself. As an individual, it's out of reach. *Koinonia* can be experienced only with other believers. The Holy Spirit, therefore, is primarily a shared experience. We often think of the Holy Spirit as a Person to be encountered as an individual. But in the New Testament, the outpouring of the Spirit is virtually always given in the context of a shared-life community where other believers are actively involved.

Certainly, there are individual spiritual experiences. But normative spiritual encounters are those that we receive with and in the body of Christ. This is the meaning of *koinonia*.

In its highest expression, *koinonia* takes place among a shared-life community. *Koinonia*, however, can devolve into something quite pathological and poisonous. It can become koinonitis.

Koinonitis is the unhealthy overabundance of fellowship that turns a church into an insular, ingrown, self-absorbed community. Koinonitis is too much of a good thing. It's "fellowship inflammation."

Like high blood pressure, koinonitis is a symptomless disease. A church is typically unaware of it until it suffers a stroke. Outsiders, however, can spot it immediately. Here are eight characteristics of this disease:

1. The church becomes little more than a Christian ghetto. It has unwittingly built an impenetrable wall of protection around itself. Relationships become deified to the point where members don't feel comfortable having anyone else included who differs in mind-set, belief, or jargon.

2. Even though the church desires to grow, in reality, it has an us-four-and-no-more mentality. It has devolved into an ingrown toenail—an exclusive huddle of navel-gazers who are shortsighted by the view of their own bellies.

3. The church exists solely for itself and its members. It may claim that it exists for the Lord, but in reality it has become a self-enclosed universe. (This universe may also include other churches that are part of the group's sectarian movement.)

4. There is little-to-no numerical growth in the church over the long haul. Most people who visit feel awkward and out of place. More leave than stay. The church can go on for years with little-to-no growth, yet few members wince. The thought never occurs to them that *they* may have something to do with the low volume.

5. A sense of cliquishness is noticeable by those on the outside. Visitors feel *welcome* to attend meetings, but they don't feel *wanted*. The church views them as intruders who may fracture the established fellowship.

6. The church has absolutely no impact on the surrounding culture. Because the members are so absorbed with one another, they never reach outside their four walls. They have little-to-no concern for the lost. They are neither salt nor light to their community. The group can go on for a decade without leading one lost soul to Christ.

7. The church operates on an out-of-sight-out-of-mind basis. People who leave or relocate are erased from the church's memory banks.

8. The church is monumentally disinterested in what the Lord is doing in other churches and in other Christians outside their circle. They are more interested in telling visitors what they're about rather than learning what God is doing in the visitor's life.

What is the cure for this epidemic? I know of none except a mirror. Koinonitis is like acne. You can't see it unless someone can manage to show you your own reflection.

Koinonitis is a highly contagious STD—a spiritually transmitted disease. Consequently, if you remain part of a church that suffers from it, you will become infected yourself.

Remember the Lord's word to the church in Laodicea in Revelation 3:17. He essentially says, "You say that you are rich. You say that you have need of nothing. But you don't realize that you are poor, blind, and naked."

In John 15, Jesus likens Himself and the church as a vine tree. If you look at any vine, the branches extend outward as the tree grows. So long as the tree is growing outwardly, it will live and continue to grow. But if it grows inwardly, it will die. Jesus Christ is the Vine, and we are the branches. His nature is to grow outwardly.

Like any fatal disease, early prevention is essential to curing koinonitis. Interestingly, both the prevention and the treatment for koinonitis is the same: *a blood transfusion.*

The chief passion of our Lord is to have a bride who loves Him, a house that suits Him, a body that expresses Him, and a family that enjoys Him. But where does He obtain His bride, His house, His body, and His family?

From the world.

God loves the world. His kingdom has come to this world.

After we've become Christians for any length of time, it's easy to forget that we were once in the world and that we found the Lord through someone else.

Recall that when Paul planted a few churches in the major cities

of a province, he considered the entire province to be evangelized
(Rom. 16:1–27). Indeed, Paul had built into the foundation of the
church God's heart for the world. As a result, the churches eventually
multiplied organically and in season.

I'm no fan of modern forms of evangelism. In my experience,
most are duty driven, guilt based, and riddled with the language
of war, conquest, courtroom battle, and hard-sell salesmanship. As
a result, they often do more harm than good. But a church that
touches the heart of Jesus will seek fresh ways to expose Him to the
lost and make Him as attractive as He is in reality.

In the first century, people were captured by seeing the church in
action. This is because they lived by an indwelling Lord and carried
on His earthly ministry. They also loved one another in a way that
trumped anything that the world had ever seen.

Therefore, the best thing your church can do to prevent koinonitis
is to explore ways of naturally developing relationships with lost
people and seek new ways of telling your story to them. Also, the
gospel that's presented in action, through works of compassion,
healing, love, and concern for others, is far more effective than giving
people the "plan of salvation." In the words of Francis of Assisi,
"Preach the gospel always, and when necessary use words."

As an aside, I would encourage you to discuss practical ways
that your church can make people feel not only welcomed, but
also wanted. Seek to identify those things that turn people off and
that discourage them from wanting to visit again. In that regard, it
wouldn't be a bad idea to survey those visitors who never end up
returning. Ask them to honestly tell you what they didn't like about
their experience with the group.

While the church of Jesus Christ should never be *attractional* in the sense of creating programs and schemes to attract Christians and non-Christians, it certainly should be *attractive*. The reason being that her Lord, who embodies the church, is the most attractive and glorious Person in the universe. When she, the *ekklesia*, is following her spiritual instincts, she makes Christ visible. And people are drawn to Him through her testimony. That testimony includes her corporate meetings as well as her community life (1 Cor. 14:23–25).

Finally, expose yourself to ministries that are outward focused and have a heart for the world.

Spiritual Myopia

Another ecclesiological malignancy is what I call "spiritual myopia." Myopia is nearsightedness. If you are myopic, you can only see those things that are close to you. Everything else is a blur. Spiritual myopia sets in when a church cannot see past a certain point and is blinded to the big picture.

There's a story in Joshua 3 that illustrates this disease very well. When Israel journeyed in the wilderness, God led them by the ark of the covenant. God's people followed the ark, which was carried on the shoulders of the priests.

The Lord told Israel to always keep their distance from the ark—at least a thousand yards away. The reason: If they got too close to the ark, they would "lose their way." The Lord was saying, "Do not get too close to the ark, or else you will get off track. You will get lost. You will be thrown off course."

God wanted Israel to walk far away enough from the ark so that they could see the ark. But also, so that they could see everything else in proportion to it.

Oftentimes nontraditional churches become fixated on a certain practice, a certain doctrine, or a certain truth, and they can't see past it. The result: Everything is out of proportion, and the church loses its direction. It becomes a lost ball in high weeds. This is spiritual myopia.

"Do not get too close to the ark. Keep things in proportion. Keep them in perspective. Back off, and see the big picture." That's what Joshua 3 teaches us.

The big picture is God's eternal purpose in Christ—the *Missio Dei*. Christ is the center of that purpose. Thus, He is the focus of our meetings. He is the subject of our conversations, our concentration, our sharing, our songs, and our fellowship.

Christ alone.

When something other than Christ takes center stage in the life of a church, it has contracted spiritual myopia. The church gets derailed from its proper center. It doesn't exist for God's ageless purpose, but for something lower.

Like koinonitis, those who suffer from spiritual myopia are typically unaware that they have it. Here are four symptoms for diagnosis:

1. The church's gatherings revolve around a special doctrine or practice. In every meeting, the same stanza is sung over and over. The same tape is played and replayed. The same chord is strung and restrung.

Every time the church comes together—some "thing" governs the meeting. It could be homeschooling, or a certain view of end times, or a certain set of doctrines. The issue gets preeminent airplay in the meetings.

Visitors who are interested in joining the group will be quizzed at some point to see where they stand on the cherished issue.

2. The people who make up the church do not perceive themselves to be anything other than Christ-centered. But people on the outside can quickly identify the hobbyhorse that the church is riding.

3. Like koinonitis, spiritual myopia inhibits outward growth. Those who join the group are people who share the church's favorite "issue." If they do not, they are either proselytized to it or they're made to feel unwelcomed. The church is little more than a special-interest group. Those who end up belonging must share the special interest.

4. Spiritual myopia fosters churches that are full of haughty bluster. Such pride translates into the death knell of the community. In the church's eyes, they lack nothing spiritually. But in the Lord's eyes, they lack greatly. The net effect is that the Lord will withdraw from the group. He will "remove your lampstand from its place" (assuming that it existed in the first place—Rev. 2:5).

Anytime a group of Christians meets on the basis of a certain doctrine or practice, it's doomed before it begins. At some point, it will be headed toward disintegration or an agonizing split.

Consider for a moment: What happens when some begin to question the cherished doctrine or practice? What if someone starts challenging the party line? Such questions and challenges will cut straight to the heart of the foundation of the group. And the members will be headed toward the battlefield.

Jesus Christ is the only true foundation for a church. Thus, a groundbreaking revelation of Him in His fullness is good medicine for this illness. It's also the best preventative measure. No hobbyhorse doctrine or cherished practice can survive in the presence of an unveiling of Christ. So find those who have ministries that are centered on Christ. (But be sure that they aren't legalistic, elitist, or sectarian; if they are, they will hurt the church.) Invite them in for a weekend, and let them preach Christ until the church is awash with His glory, and He alone becomes your controlling vision.

CHAPTER 22

THE DISEASES OF AN ORGANIC CHURCH II

> *Then I said to them, "You see the trouble we are in:*
> *Jerusalem lies in ruins, and its gates have been burned*
> *with fire. Come, let us rebuild the wall of Jerusalem,*
> *and we will no longer be in disgrace."*

—Nehemiah in Nehemiah 2:17

The third disease that wreaks havoc on organic churches is what I call "spiritual dwarfism." We have an organ in our brain called the pituitary gland. It's also known as the master gland, and it's responsible for physical growth. If that organ is deformed or malfunctions, it will stunt a person's growth. Experts call it "pituitary dwarfism."

Spiritual Dwarfism

Spiritual dwarfism is the arrested spiritual development of a church. When a church is inflicted with this crippling disease, its spiritual growth is retarded, and it experiences spiritual inertia. Four symptoms for diagnosis are as follows:

1. Only a few people function when the church gathers. The rest are passive spectators. Note: One of the marks of a spiritual babe is that they always need to have predigested food dished out to them. They are always receiving and never giving.

2. There is virtually no spiritual depth to what's shared in the meetings. People talk about "things"—religious things, biblical things, even spiritual things. But there is hardly anything said that reflects a living and experiential knowledge of the Lord. What is shared is shallow, superficial, and surface. It may be intellectually and theologically stimulating, but it's spiritually empty and colorless. Put another way, the group thrives on milk. There is an absence of solid spiritual food.

3. The believers never talk about the Lord outside of scheduled meetings. There is no handling of Christ during the week. The only time He gets any airtime at all is when the church gathers together. And even then it's quite minimal.

4. The root cause of this malady is malnutrition. To paraphrase the prophet Amos, "There is a famine in the church; not of one of food or water, but of hearing the Lord's word" (Amos 8:11).

The prevention and treatment for this sickness is a steady diet of strong spiritual meat. Exposure to ministries that can feed the church with spiritual meat (the deeper things of Christ) and teach it how to feed itself is vital.

Another healthy prescription is to invite another organic church (one that is mature and healthy) to have a weekend spiritual retreat with the members of your church.

Hyperpneumia

Pneuma is the Greek word for "spirit." *Hyper* means "too much." Hyperpneumia is an unhealthy focus on the miraculous activity of the Holy Spirit. Churches that are pathologically obsessed with supernatural phenomena and demonstrations of the miraculous suffer from this disease. Here are four symptoms:

1. The members seek signs and wonders right up to the Adam's apple.

2. In every meeting, each member seeks to get his or her own individual needs met by the supernatural workings of the Holy Spirit. They show up to meetings like empty buckets expecting to be filled. They come expecting a feeling, a sign, a wonder, a miracle, a personal word of prophecy, etc.

3. The church becomes completely dependent on meetings where each person is praying and prophesying over one another. If this doesn't happen, the meeting is regarded as a failure, and members conclude that the Holy Spirit wasn't present.

4. When the hype fades and the phenomenological experiences begin to wane, members feel that something is amiss. Their faith takes a dive. They grow bored with the gatherings. They either try to pump up the gifts of the Spirit in the energy of human emotion, or they conclude that God has given up on the group. Some will pack their bags and go elsewhere to find where "the Holy Spirit is moving." (This becomes a never-ending cycle in the lives of some Christians.)

The prevention and treatment for hyperpneumia is to discover and explore the interior Christian life. The remedy is found in understanding the difference between an indwelling Lord and the outward power of the Spirit. It's in learning the difference between the felt presence of God and the awareness of God's presence.

In cases where this disease has become terminal, the remedy is to drop everything, clear the decks, and start all over again. Only this time, everyone in the group should take time to learn how to become nonreligious (see part 3). Each person's concepts of spiritual gifts should be laid down at the cross of Christ. The whole church should take a vacation from exercising spiritual gifts and learn Jesus Christ like newborn babes. That's one sure way to kill the virus.[1]

Plan for Prevention

It's far wiser to prevent an illness than to cure one after contracting it. What follows, then, are three important ingredients for building a healthy immune system. Each one represents a long-term regimen for good health.

Eating the right food. The church must learn how to draw its life and energy from nothing but Jesus Christ (John 6:57). If an organic church doesn't know how to do this, it will not survive spiritually (though it may continue to meet). It must learn to nourish itself with those things that are invisible and intangible. In addition, it must receive a balanced meal. The riches of Christ are infinite in scope. If a church partakes of only one or two aspects of Him, it will become undernourished and deformed. Old Testament Israel could sustain the manna for only so long. They were meant to live off all the riches in the land of Canaan.

---

1   For details see "Stripping Down to Christ Alone: Rethinking the Gifts of the Spirit" at: www.ptmin.org/gifts.pdf.

Regular exercise. Nourishing oneself with spiritual food is not enough. The church must share its spiritual food with its members. That is, the members must function in the meetings. They must learn to partake of Christ individually and corporately and then impart His life to the other members in the gatherings. Such spiritual functioning is the lifeblood of an organic church.

Obtain a health practitioner. In the first century, itinerant workers were given to the church by God to show the Lord's people how to draw their spiritual supply from Christ. They also helped them to spot those spiritual maladies to which they may have been blinded. If a church was suffering from a sickness, they treated it.

All of Paul's epistles were provoked by church problems. Like a fine surgeon, Paul's letters were the divine instruments by which God effected their healing. Christian workers, therefore, are servants to the body of Christ. They function as health-care practitioners, acting as spiritual nurses, doctors, nutritionists, and sometimes surgeons.

Understanding church pathology is vital for the sustained health of an organic church. Yet there's also the danger of becoming a spiritual hypochondriac. Continuous introspection is itself a sign of sickness. It prevents action. So don't make a ritual out of checking your spiritual pulse. The paralysis of self-analysis can end up killing a church as well.

If you belong to an organic church, I recommend that the members come together once a year or so to take its spiritual temperature, check its pulse, and measure its vital signs. In this way, this chapter will be translated from bloodless theory into practical help—help that may just save the life of your community.

CHAPTER 23

HOW AN APOSTOLIC WORKER CARES FOR A CHURCH

A small body of determined spirits fired by an unquenchable faith in their mission can alter the course of history.

—Gandhi

Taking Paul as the model Christian worker and drawing material from the Epistles and the book of Acts, we can glean the following about how a worker nurtures a church in his care:[1]

> ❧ A worker cares for a church by spending as much time as necessary to build its foundation (1 Cor. 3:10). Note: Paul typically spent three to six months with a church on his initial visit.

---

1   The following references are based on the NASB.

This is mostly due to the fact that he was so often run out of town by his detractors. The exceptions: He spent eighteen months planting the church in Corinth and three years planting the church in Ephesus.

🌱 A worker cares for a church by visiting it (1 Thess. 2:18; 3:10; 1 Cor. 4:19; 16:6; 2 Cor. 1:15; Rom. 1:10–13; 15:22–24; Phil. 2:24). Note: A worker's visit is always designed to bring blessing to the church (2 Cor. 1:15, 24; Rom. 1:11–12; 15:29; Phil. 1:25–26).

🌱 A worker cares for a church by writing letters to it. Note: Nine of Paul's letters are written to churches, both of Peter's letters were written to churches, at least two of John's letters were written to churches, and James' and Jude's letters were written to churches. Add to this the letters mentioned in 1 Corinthians 5:11; 2 Corinthians 7:8; and Colossians 4:16.

🌱 A worker cares for a church by unveiling the glories of Christ to it (Eph. 1—3; Col. 1—2).

🌱 A worker cares for a church by exhorting and encouraging it in the Lord (Acts 14:22; 1 Thess. 2:11; 4:1; 1 Cor. 1:10; 4:16).

❧ A worker cares for a church by teaching it (1 Cor. 4:17; Col. 1:28).

❧ A worker cares for a church by admonishing and warning it when necessary (1 Thess. 2:11; 1 Cor. 4:14; Col. 1:28).

❧ A worker cares for a church by reminding it to observe important practices (1 Cor. 11:2, 23; Titus 3:1).

❧ A worker cares for a church by urging it to specific action or attitude (1 Thess. 5:14; 2 Cor. 2:8; 6:1; Rom. 12:1; 15:30; 16:17; Col. 2:16, 18; Phil. 2:18).

❧ A worker cares for a church by charging it in the Lord (1 Thess. 4:11; 5:27; 2 Thess. 3:4–6, 10–12). Note: Paul rarely did this, even though he had the spiritual authority to do so (Philem. 8–9).

❧ A worker cares for a church by charging individuals in the church to stop teaching harmful doctrines (1 Tim. 1:3).

❧ A worker cares for a church by correcting those who refuse to stop sinning (1 Tim. 5:20).

❧ A worker cares for a church by asking it to esteem those who serve it (1 Thess. 5:12–13; 1 Cor. 16:15–16; Phil. 2:29).

❧ A worker cares for a church by exhorting the church to warmly greet its members with family affection (1 Thess. 5:26; 1 Cor. 16:20; 2 Cor. 13:12; Rom. 16:16).

❧ A worker cares for a church by instructing and refuting those who introduce false teachings into it (1 Tim. 1:3; Titus 1:9).

❧ A worker cares for a church by making practical suggestions to ensure that its meetings are edifying (1 Cor. 11:33–34; 14:26–40).

❧ A worker cares for a church by giving specific direction to it (1 Cor. 16:1–3).

❧ A worker cares for a church by inquiring about its spiritual progress and well-being (1 Thess. 3:5; Phil. 2:19).

❧ A worker cares for a church by asking it to excommunicate those who refuse to stop committing certain serious sins (2 Thess. 3:14–15; 1 Cor. 5:1–7, 13).

❧ A worker cares for a church by asking other churches to help it during a crisis (Rom. 15:25–27; 1 Cor. 16:1ff.; 2 Cor. 8—9).

❧ A worker cares for a church by asking it not to gossip or speak negatively about others (Eph. 4:29, 31; Col. 4:6).

❧ A worker cares for a church by asking it to receive other brothers and sisters in the Lord (Rom. 16:1–2; Col. 4:10).

❧ A worker cares for a church by sending his coworkers to visit it when he cannot.

Examples:

❧ Paul sent Timothy to the church in Thessalonica to strengthen and encourage it during its trials (1 Thess. 3:2).

❧ Paul sent Timothy to Corinth (1 Cor. 16:10).

❧ Paul hoped to send Timothy to the church in Philippi to learn of its spiritual condition (Phil. 2:19).

❧ Paul asked Apollos to visit Corinth, but he declined (1 Cor. 16:12).

❧ Paul sent Titus to Corinth (2 Cor. 8:6, 16–17).

❧ Paul sent another brother with Titus to Corinth (2 Cor. 12:18).

❧ Paul sent Epaphroditus back to Philippi (Phil. 2:25).

- Paul left Titus in Crete and gave him instructions on how to strengthen the churches there (Titus 1:5).

- Paul sent Artemas or Tychicus to Crete to replace Titus (Titus 3:12).

- Paul sent Titus to Nicopolis (Titus 3:12).

- Paul sent Tychicus to the churches in Asia Minor to make known his condition and to encourage their hearts (Col. 4:7–8; Eph. 6:21–22).

- Paul sent Tychicus to Ephesus again (2 Tim. 4:12).

CHAPTER 24

THE JOURNEY AHEAD

Is there another stream running even more deeply and more hiddenly these days among the members of the Body, a scattered people who are being taken into the depths of the revelation and experience of Christ in the most extreme measures of the Holy Spirit's dealings, emptying, crucifying ... a pioneer company which the Lord will need for the opening of the way for the remainder of the Body to follow—perhaps some "eleventh-hour laborers" now in the process of His producing?

—George Moreshead

The divine principle of extralocal, itinerant work is the forgotten chapter in the first-century story. It's the overlooked pattern of the New Testament narrative. It's the neglected ministry of the body of Christ.

If we will see a richer and higher expression of the body of Christ, it's our responsibility to return to first principles. If we do not, God's timeless purpose will continue to suffer loss. Doubtlessly, we will continue to see many small bands of Christians seeking to meet organically, but many—if not most—will be shallow and unsustainable.

I believe that the need of the hour is for Christians who are called by God to raise up the church as a living, breathing experience. Christians who are broken and tested. Christians who refuse to take shortcuts but who have *first* lived in an organic expression of body life as brothers and sisters before they ever dare plant a church. Christians who have a deep and living relationship with Jesus Christ. Christians whose lives have been devastated by the cross and the breaking of God. Christians who have incomparable insight into the mystery of God. Christians whose only passion is the Lord and His house. Christians who have a revelation of Christ that burns in their bosom. Christians who are mesmerized by the face of God, and who have the ability to preach Christ in such profound depths that God's people are left staggering.

The need of the hour is for such people to wait on God until they are properly prepared and then sent. And once sent, to plant the church in the same way that all first-century workers did: by equipping it and then abandoning it to the Holy Spirit.

Equally needed is for the body of Christ to recognize the role of such people.

Today is a day of repairing and mending. And repairing the corporate testimony of God's people is no small thing. While there is no shortage of Christians in the West, there is a great dearth in the way of corporate testimony. God's grand mission is to secure a people in every locale that are foundationally constituted and built together as a visible, locatable, geographical, corporate expression of His Son.

Christians who have left the institutional church, no matter how long they have been saved, will have an awfully hard time going on with other Christians in a face-to-face community without a clergy. Thus, workers who know the headship of Christ—who have experienced genuine body life with all of its glory and gore and who have been broken by God's sovereign dealings—are an indispensable resource for helping God's people discover how to gather under Christ's direct headship today.

Exploring Your Options

Organic church life is relatively easy to discover. It occurs all over this planet. Whenever Christians gather in an informal way without static ritual and experience the living Christ together, body life begins. But it does not last long. So having organic church life is easy if the right ingredients are in place. But it's extremely difficult to keep alive and pure.

For this reason, both Scripture and experience testify that the aid of an itinerant worker is a net plus in the whole operation of organic church life. Critics may misconstrue this candid observation as job security for modern apostles. (The workers I know do not charge for their spiritual service. Unlike most ministers today, they come free.) It's just the raw fact. And to my mind, it represents an urgent need that exists in the kingdom of God today. On the heels of that, what follows are my suggestions to the following groups of people.

TO THOSE CALLED TO CHURCH PLANTING

You have two main options as far as I'm concerned. That is, if you wish to be on scriptural grounds:

1. Give up your ambition and your pride. Surrender your lust for position, humble yourself, and relocate to where there's a genuine organic expression of the church. And live in that church as a nonleader for a period of years.

Learn Jesus Christ all over again in the context of body life. Even better, if you can find such a rare thing on this earth, move to a city where an experienced, honest, nonlegalistic, nonelitist, and nonsectarian church planter is actively raising up a church. Watch him explode with spiritual passion as he builds the house of the living God, and learn all you can from him.

If you are truly called by the Lord to raise up His house, this is your lineage. Every church planter in the New Testament walked this path.

2. If it is impossible for you to move, your other option is to invite a church planter to your town to raise up a church. You, of course, would simply be a brother or a sister in that church with no special status. As we saw in part 1, this is God's way of raising up Christian workers.

TO YOUNG MEN AND WOMEN WHO FEEL CALLED OF GOD

In my personal judgment, those who are called of the Lord should not begin their ministries before the age of thirty. This principle is consistent throughout Scripture. Priests were trained for their ministry in their twenties, and they began their service at age thirty (Num.

4:3ff.). Jesus Christ, the model for all church planters, did not begin His ministry until He was thirty years of age (Luke 3:23).

There are pragmatic reasons for this. People in their twenties have simply not lived long enough to acquire the wisdom necessary to handle the enormous and monumental problems that will arise in church life. They have not yet learned the depths of the cross or of Jesus Christ Himself.

In addition, youthful enthusiasm is a powerful counterfeit for genuine loyalty to the Lord and the power of God. It's also commonly exploited by religious organizations. In their excitement, young people don't just jump on the horse; they jump over it. And when they hit thirty, or close to it, they often burn out.

I've met many Christians in their late twenties and early thirties who had expended their youth on some Christian organization. Sadly, their enthusiasm for God drained away. Their adrenals had been beaten to death. Their Christian life had been wrung dry.

The engine of youthful enthusiasm will run only so long. Then it crashes and burns. While it looks like the power of God at first glance, it's a human substitute. In this connection, countless young men and women who were ready to die for Christ in their early twenties have fallen away from Him when they neared the age of thirty.

In her timeless classic *Passages*, Gail Sheehy demonstrates that during the ages of eighteen to twenty-two, people are seeking a hero—a mentor to follow. They are also avidly searching for a cause greater than themselves to throw their lives into. It's for this reason that many Christians were converted between the ages of eighteen and twenty-two. They don't realize that they are doing this at the time, but during those ages, they are exploring their options for life.

When a person reaches the ages of twenty-eight through thirty-two, however, they begin to question and reappraise every major commitment they made in their twenties. Those commitments are either abandoned or deepened. It is for this reason that many who hit age thirty end up tearing up the lives that they built during their twenties. That includes shedding themselves of their mentor (in some cases, they turn against them). Sheehy calls this the "Catch-30" crisis. Illusions are shaken. It's the time to break or deepen commitments—to dig in or bail out.

I have lost count of the number of people I knew in their twenties who loved the Lord passionately and would seemingly do anything to serve Him. Yet when they hit thirty, those same people turned their backs on God and elected to no longer be invested in the Christian faith. The embers of youthful zeal died out; the engine that had run their spiritual lives skid to a screeching halt. And there was nothing left for them to run on.

For this reason, people who are called of God to His work ought to spend their twenties experiencing Christ and the life of the church. They ought to discover the work of the cross and the basic lessons of living by divine life. They should wait on their ministry and not hurry it.

So I ask: Can you, young man or woman, wait on your ministry? Can you throw away the clock, forget the calendar, and give up your lust for serving God? And instead, get to know Him first—deeply—in the context of Christian community?

Only then will you be of use in helping to fulfill God's eternal purpose. Without an experience of the cross and knowing Jesus Christ in authentic, organic community, you will not have the proper preparation to raise up the house of the living God.

TO PASTORS WHO WISH TO MAKE THE TRANSITION

As I have said elsewhere, transitioning from an institutional church to an organic church is not cosmetic surgery. It's a complete overhaul. I cannot give specific advice on how to do this in a book because each institutional church has a varying set of elements. (For instance, some own buildings, some do not. Some have hired clergy, some have not. Some are megachurches, while some are very small, etc.) But I can give you a few general suggestions that will furnish you with a beginning:

1. Shut down your Sunday-morning and Wednesday-evening "services." Instead, have a Wednesday-evening "ministry meeting." Begin these meetings as you would ordinarily begin your church services, with worship and praise through music and song.

You will not be giving your typical sermons in these meetings. The purpose of these meetings is to change the paradigm that's present in your congregation. Your short-term goal is to give them a vision of God's eternal purpose and their place in it.

Many pastors are gifted teachers. So I would encourage you to begin teaching through one of the books under "The Mission of God" section listed on the site www.HouseChurchResource.org.[1] The other thing you will want to do in these "ministry meetings" has to do with the next point.

2. On Sunday mornings, the congregation will meet in homes. They will divide up into these homes ranging from twelve to twenty people. The divisions will be determined by geography. In these home

---

1   *Ultimate Intention, From Eternity to Here,* and *The Stewardship of the Mystery* have been the most popular for this exercise. *From Eternity* has a free discussion guide at www.FromEternityToHere.org.

meetings (not services), each group will go through the assignments in part 3 of this book.

Important: There will be no designated leaders or facilitators in these home meetings. It's your job to equip the congregation on how to go through these assignments. And to get weekly reports on how things are going. You can make time for these "reports" during your Wednesday-evening "ministry meetings."

So you will have two meetings a week. One will be the "ministry meeting," where you will teach through a book; the other will be home meetings, where the congregation will go through the assignments in part 3 of this book.

3. Once each group has completed each of the assignments in part 3, invite an experienced church planter to hold a weekend conference for your congregation. The church planter will then make suggestions regarding the next step. Let me stress that the above three points are only the beginning of the transition.

A Challenge We Must Face

I sincerely hope that every person engaged in church planting would face the enormity of their task. So many have taken shortcuts in their preparation. So many have adopted nonbiblical methods for starting churches. So many have never experienced organic church life or allowed themselves to be deeply known by others in Christian community. So many have simply not bled enough. This is the great tragedy of the present-day Christian worker.

Perhaps this book will awaken some out of their daydream of wrongly assuming that the church of Jesus Christ is something cheap and easy to build.

It's my sincere conviction that most of what we produce in the way of church life simply does not stack up to anything worthy of the name of the bride of Christ or the house of God. Many in our day have a rather anemic view of the church. They see it as a voluntary association of the saved. Either that or they view it as the equivalent of human relationships, a Bible study, or an evangelistic mission.

But the church is so much more than that. Therefore, I wish to raise your standard of what the church is according to the heart and mind of God. As I've demonstrated in *From Eternity to Here,* the church is both divine and human, heavenly and earthly, spiritual and natural. It's the corporate expression of Jesus Christ worked out in a close-knit community of human beings.

To bottom-line this, I believe we have started in the wrong place. And it is high time that we take pains to correct our course and return to the principle of the organic. The church of Jesus Christ is a living, breathing organism. As such, she has a right to be born in a manger, not welded together in a laboratory or sewn up in a factory. If we will see church life that fulfills the vision of God, we must return to the biblical pattern for church planting and nurturing.

For this reason, the earth awaits those whom God has called to be humble enough to learn from those who are ahead of them. It awaits those of apostolic stature who have the house of the living God on their hearts. It awaits those who are willing to align themselves with the Lord's pattern for spiritual preparation and refuse to cut corners. It awaits a day when such people will burn for God's eternal purpose and pay any price to fulfill it.

May God send that day upon this earth.

The Making of an Apostle

The kingdom of God is in desperate need of a new kind of Christian worker. A worker who is honest, nonlegalistic, nonelitist, nonsectarian, nonreligious, and who refuses to play religious games. A worker who will not fold like an accordion under the pressure of insults, ridicule, criticism, false rumor, character smears, spin, and slander, but one who can survive fire. A worker who is not in the ministry for money, game, or fame, but who serves the Lord day and night, spilling his insides, giving and dying for the kingdom of God.

There is a revolution brewing in the body of Christ today, and the need of the hour is for God to raise up, from the soil of organic church life, workers who will lead the charge. Perhaps some who are reading that last sentence wish to know "What will it take for me to be on the front lines of that revolution?"

The answer is simple. It takes vision, insight, courage, and spiritual depth. It takes humility, maturity, genius, pain, sacrifice, and lots of rejection. It takes tenfold more problems and more heartaches than you could ever imagine that God would pour out on you. It takes the ability to see the unseen, to know the depths of the Lord Jesus and the breaking and devastation of His cross, and the ability to drown God's people with a breathtaking revelation of Christ.

That's all it takes. I hope and pray that some who are reading these words will be captured by the depth of God's ways and give themselves wholly to them. Perhaps, then, the Lord's ageless purpose will find visible expression all over this planet.

Will you be one who will accept the challenge and respond to the call?

ACKNOWLEDGMENTS

I am largely indebted to four churches in Florida whom the Lord used to teach me the lessons in this book. I am also indebted to the insights of the following pioneers: the Anabaptists, the Waldensians, the early Plymouth Brethren, the Little Flock, Roland Allen, Melvin Hodges, Watchman Nee, and T. Austin-Sparks. Finally, I wish to acknowledge the following friends of mine for their contributions in this uncommon journey: Robert Banks, Hal Miller, Stephen Kaung, DeVern Fromke, Jon Zens, Milt Rodriguez, Alan Levine, Tony Dale, Felicity Dale, and Gene Edwards.

BIBLIOGRAPHY

The following bibliography includes the principal publications cited in this book along with others that are germane to the topic.

Allen, Roland. *Missionary Methods: St. Paul's or Ours?* Grand Rapids, MI: Eerdmans, 1962.

_____. *The Spontaneous Expansion of the Church.* Grand Rapids, MI: Eerdmans, 1962.

Austin-Sparks, T. *Explanation of the Nature and History of "This Ministry."* Tulsa, OK: Emmanuel Church, 2004.

_____. *God's Spiritual House.* Shippensburg, PA: Destiny Image, 2001.

_____. *Prophetic Ministry.* Shippensburg, PA: Destiny Image, 2000.

_____. *The Stewardship of the Mystery.* Shippensburg, PA: Destiny Image, 2002.

_____. *Words of Wisdom and Revelation.* St. Charles, MO: Three Brothers, 1971.

Banks, Robert. *Paul's Idea of Community.* Peabody, MA: Hendrickson, 1994.

Brock, Charles. *The Principles and Practice of Indigenous Church Planting.* Nashville, TN: Broadman Press, 1981.

Bruce, A. B. *The Training of the Twelve.* Grand Rapids, MI: Kregel, 2000.

Bruce, F. F. *Paul, Apostle of the Heart Set Free.* Grand Rapids, MI: Eerdmans, 2000.

_____. *The Book of the Acts (Revised): New International Commentary on the New Testament.* Grand Rapids, MI: Eerdmans, 1988.

_____. *The Pauline Circle.* Grand Rapids, MI: Eerdmans, 1985.

Coleman, Robert. *The Master Plan of Evangelism*. Grand Rapids, MI: Revell, 1993.

Conybeare, W. J., and J. S. Howson. *The Life and Epistles of St. Paul.* Grand Rapids, MI: Eerdmans, 1966.

Edwards, Gene. *Overlooked Christianity*, Sargent, GA: Seedsowers, 1997.

_____. *The Americanization of Christianity*, Sargent, GA: Seedsowers, 1994.

Fromke, DeVern. *Ultimate Intention*. Indianapolis, IN: Sure Foundation, 1963.

Grenz, Stanley. *Theology for the Community of God*. Grand Rapids, MI: Eerdmans, 1994.

Guthrie, Donald. *The Apostles*. Grand Rapids, MI: Zondervan, 1975.

Hay, Alexander. *The New Testament Order for Church and Missionary.* Audubon, NJ: The New Testament Missionary Union, 1947.

Hodges, Melvin. *A Guide to Church Planting*. Chicago: Moody Press, 1973.

Latham, Henry. *Pastor Pastorum or The Schooling of the Apostles by Our Lord.* New York: J. Pott, 1899.

McBirnie, William S. *The Search for the Early Church*. Wheaton, IL: Tyndale, 1978.

_____. *The Search for the Twelve Apostles*. Carol Stream, IL: Tyndale, 1973, pp. 27–28.

Murray, Stuart. *Church Planting: Laying Foundations*. Scottdale, PA: Herald Press, 2001.

Nee, Watchman. *Church Affairs*. Richmond, VA: Christian Fellowship Publishers, 1982.

_____. *The Normal Christian Church Life*. Anaheim, CA: Living Stream Ministry, 1980.

_____. *The Character of God's Workman*. Richmond, VA: Christian Fellowship Publishers, 1988.

_____. *The Ministry of God's Word.* Richmond, VA: Christian Fellowship Publishers, 1971.

_____. *The Release of the Spirit.* Indianapolis, IN: Sure Foundation, 1965.

Niebuhr, H. Richard, and Daniel D. Williams, ed. *The Ministry in Historical Perspective.* New York: Harper & Brothers, 1956.

Pinnock, Clark. *Flame of Love: A Theology of the Holy Spirit.* Downers Grove, IL: InterVarsity Press, 1996.

Robinson, John A. T. *The New Reformation?* Philadelphia: Westminster Press, 1965.

Sanday, William, and Arthur Headlam. *A Critical and Exegetical Commentary on the Epistle to the Romans.* New York: Charles Scribner's Sons, 1905.

Shenk, David, and Ervin Stutzman. *Creating Communities of the Kingdom.* Scottdale, PA: Herald Press, 1988.

Snyder, Howard. *The Community of the King.* Downers Grove, IL: InterVarsity Press, 1977.

_____. *Decoding the Church: Mapping the DNA of Christ's Body.* Grand Rapids, MI: Baker Books, 2002.

Stevens, R. Paul. *Liberating the Laity.* Vancouver, Canada: Regent Publishing, 2002.

_____. *The Abolition of the Laity.* Carlisle, PA: Paternoster Press, 1999.

Viola, Frank. *Bethany.* Gainesville, FL: Present Testimony Ministry, 2007.

_____. *From Eternity to Here.* Colorado Springs, CO: David C. Cook, 2009.

_____. *Reimagining Church.* Colorado Springs, CO: David C. Cook, 2008.

_____. *The Untold Story of the New Testament Church.* Shippensburg, PA: Destiny Image, 2004.

Viola, Frank, and George Barna. *Pagan Christianity.* Carol Stream, IL: Tyndale, 2008.

ABOUT THE AUTHOR

FRANK VIOLA is a frequent conference speaker and author of numerous books on the deeper Christian life and radical church restoration. His books include *Pagan Christianity,* coauthored with George Barna, *From Eternity to Here, Reimagining Church,* and *The Untold Story of the New Testament Church.* Frank's Web site, www.FrankViola.com, contains many free resources that will help you implement the insights in this book, including audio messages, an interactive blog, a monthly eNewsletter, articles, and more. Frank and his family live in Gainesville, Florida.